Paws & Beyond

Wild Friends in Bright Colors. Artistic Visions of the Animal Kingdom

Javier Sanz

If you enjoy this book, please consider leaving a positive review on Amazon.

Thank you :)

To the young explorers of the world,

May you always find joy in the flutter of a butterfly's wings, wonder in the song of a whale, and courage in the roar of a lion. Remember, the world is an endless canvas painted with mysteries, and you are the artists holding the brush.

Keep questioning, keep discovering, and most importantly, keep believing that you can be anything, do anything, and go anywhere your heart desires.

Happy exploring!

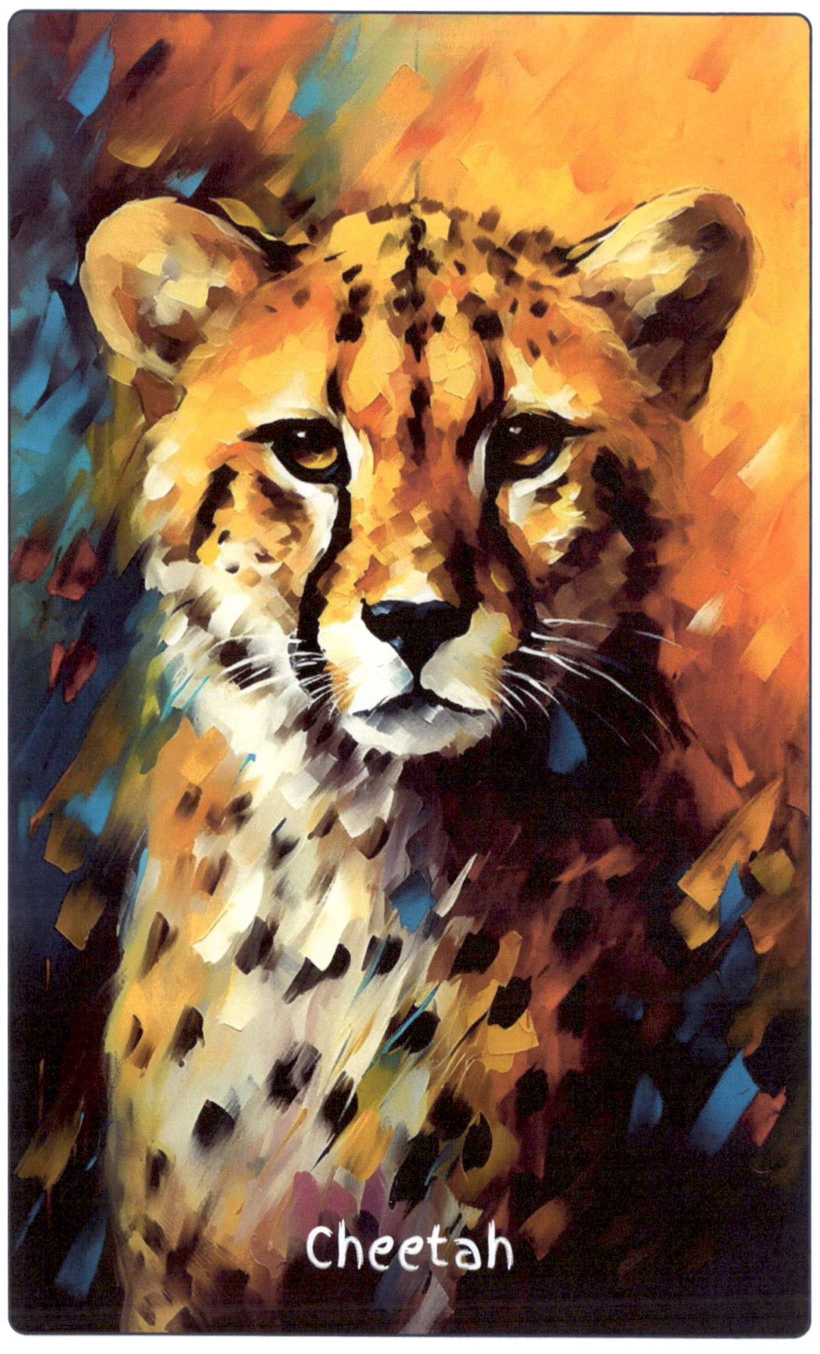

Cheetah

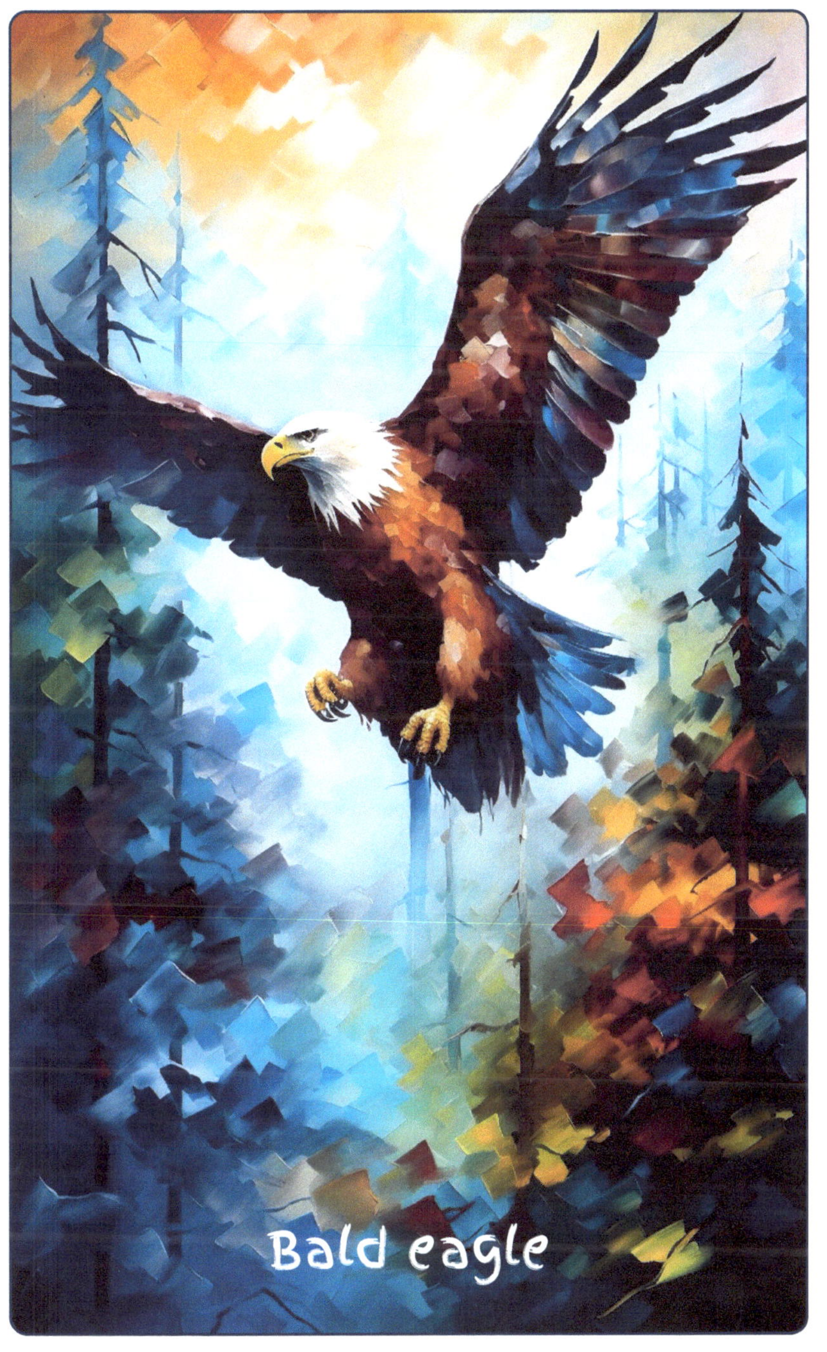

Bald eagle

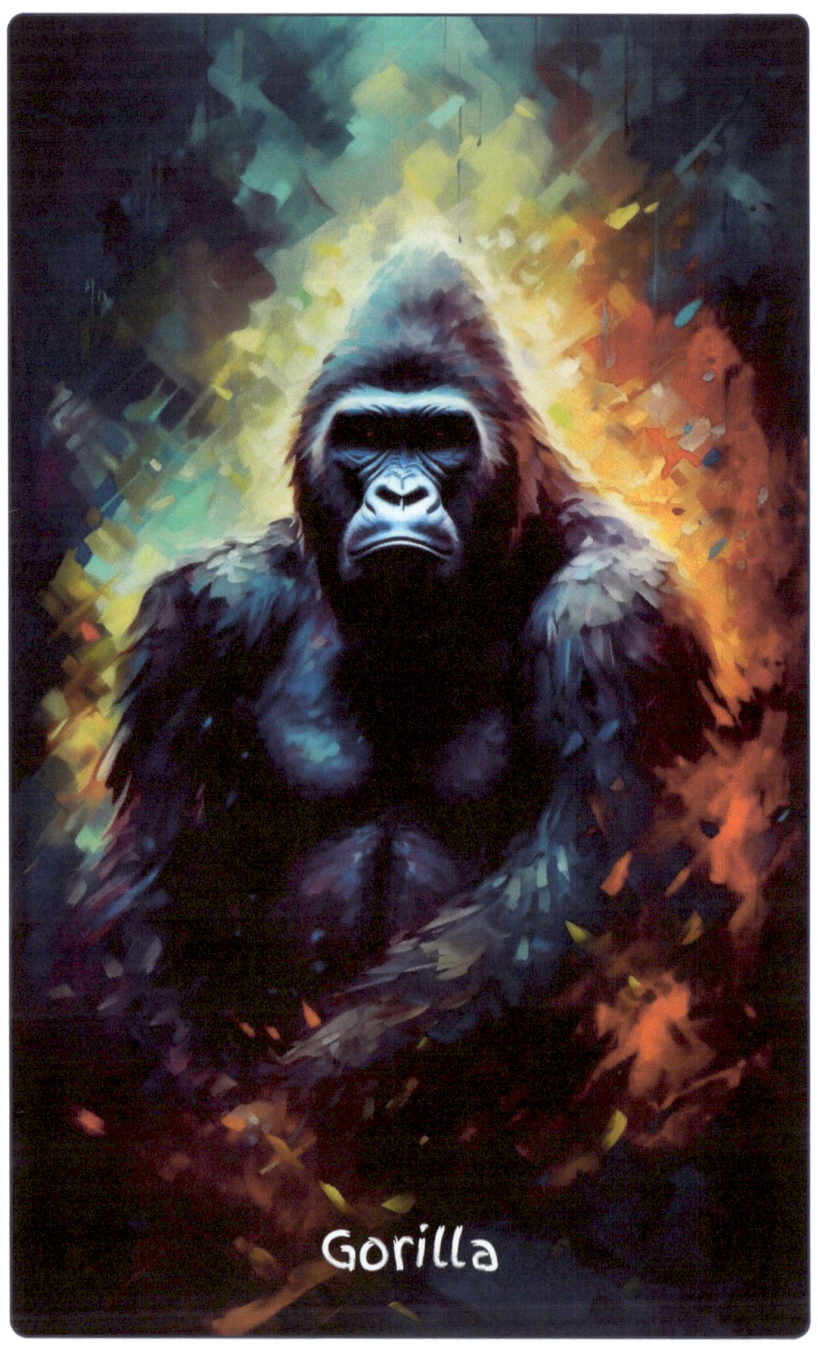

Gorilla

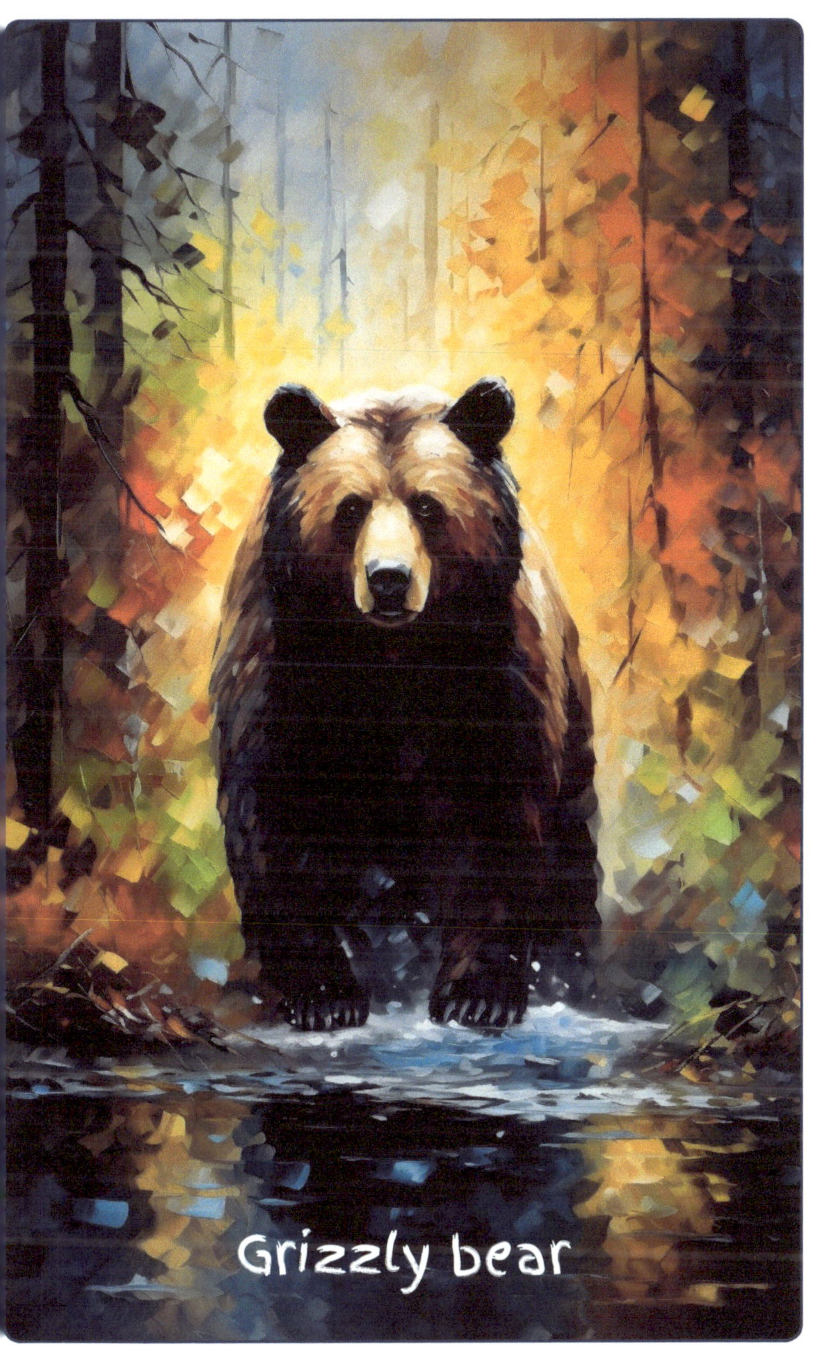

Grizzly bear

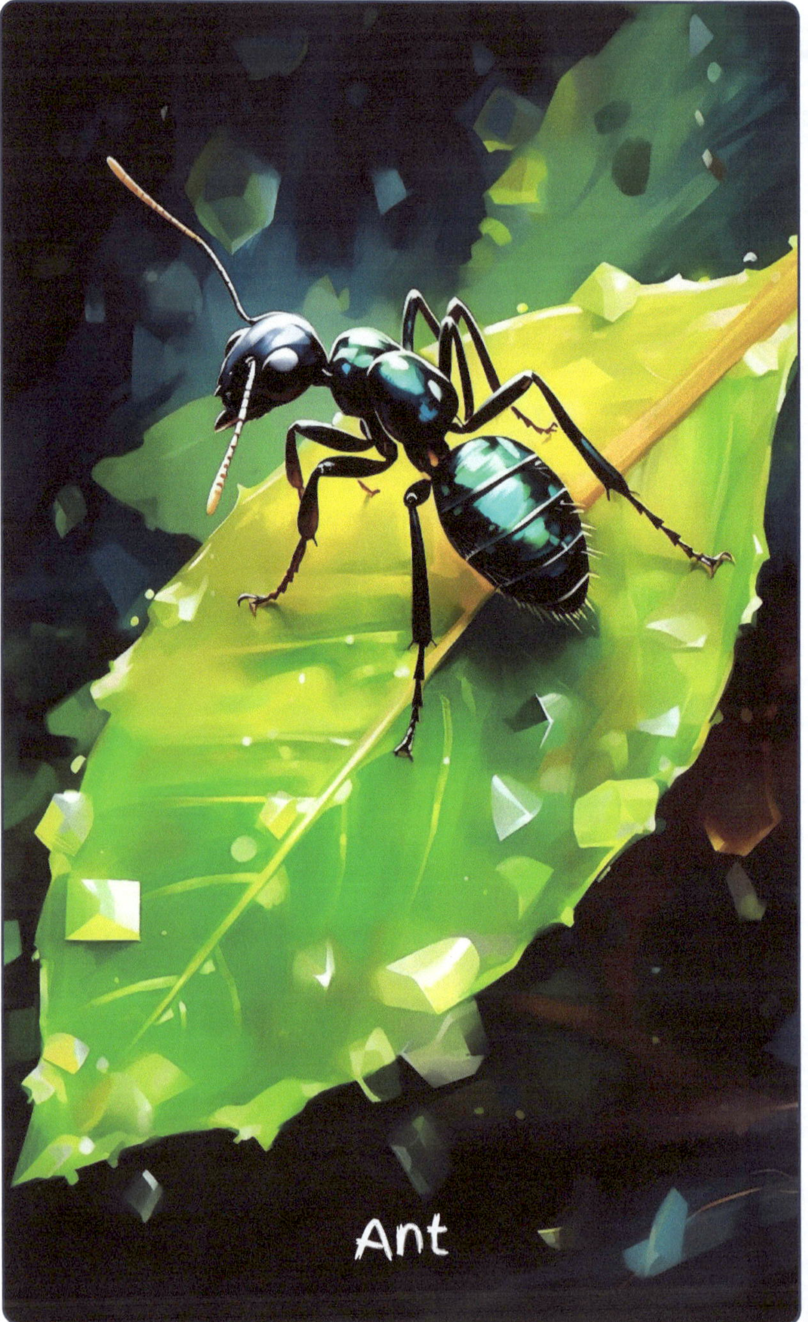

Ant

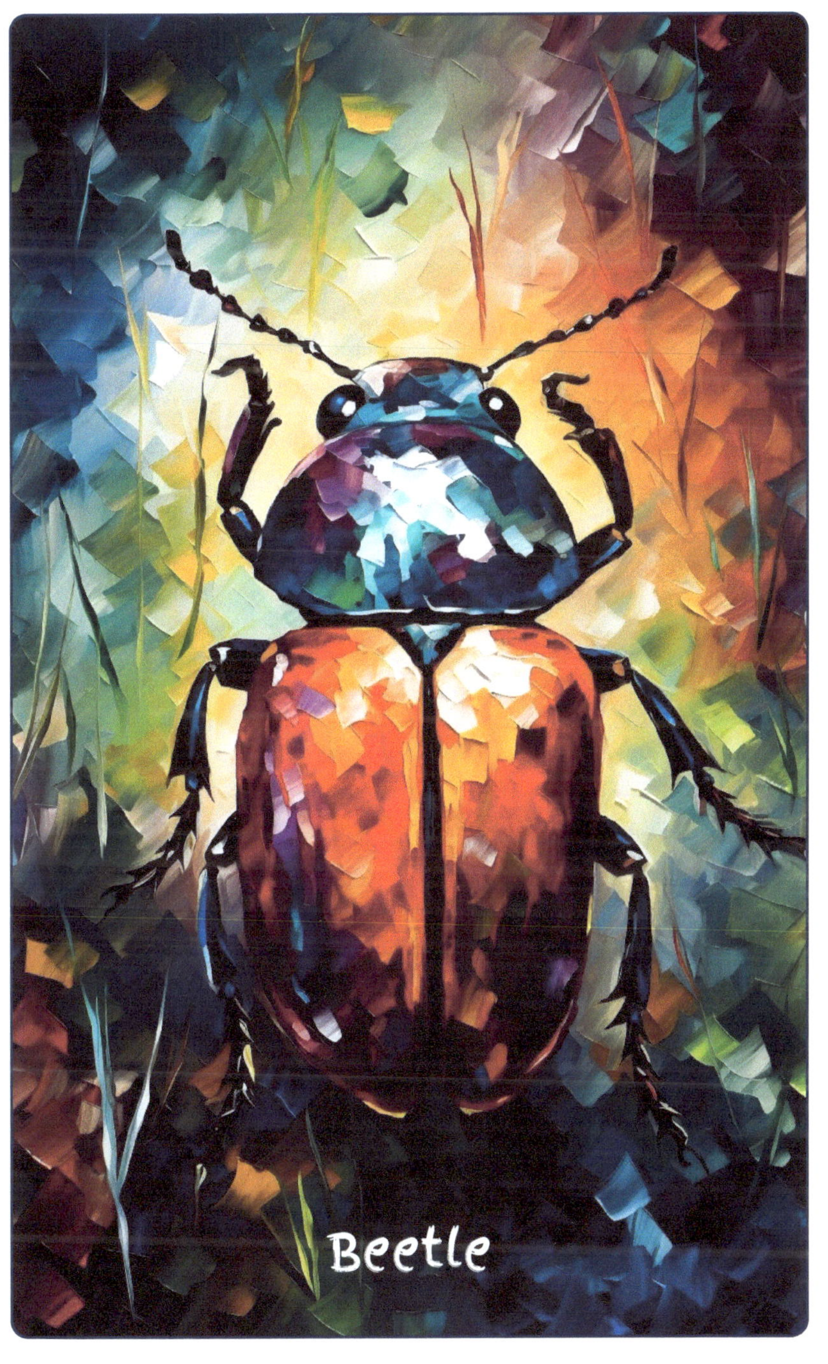

Beetle

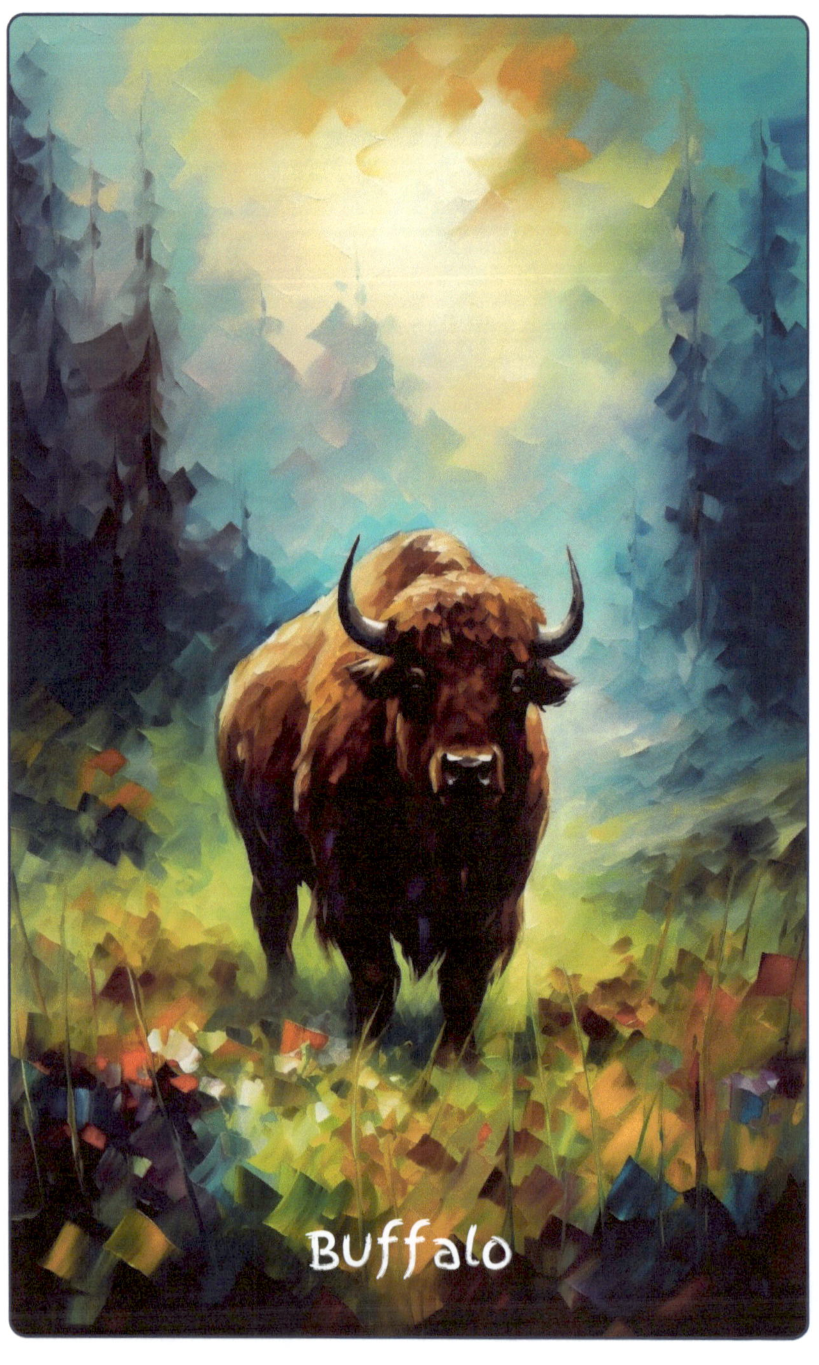
Buffalo
Buffalo

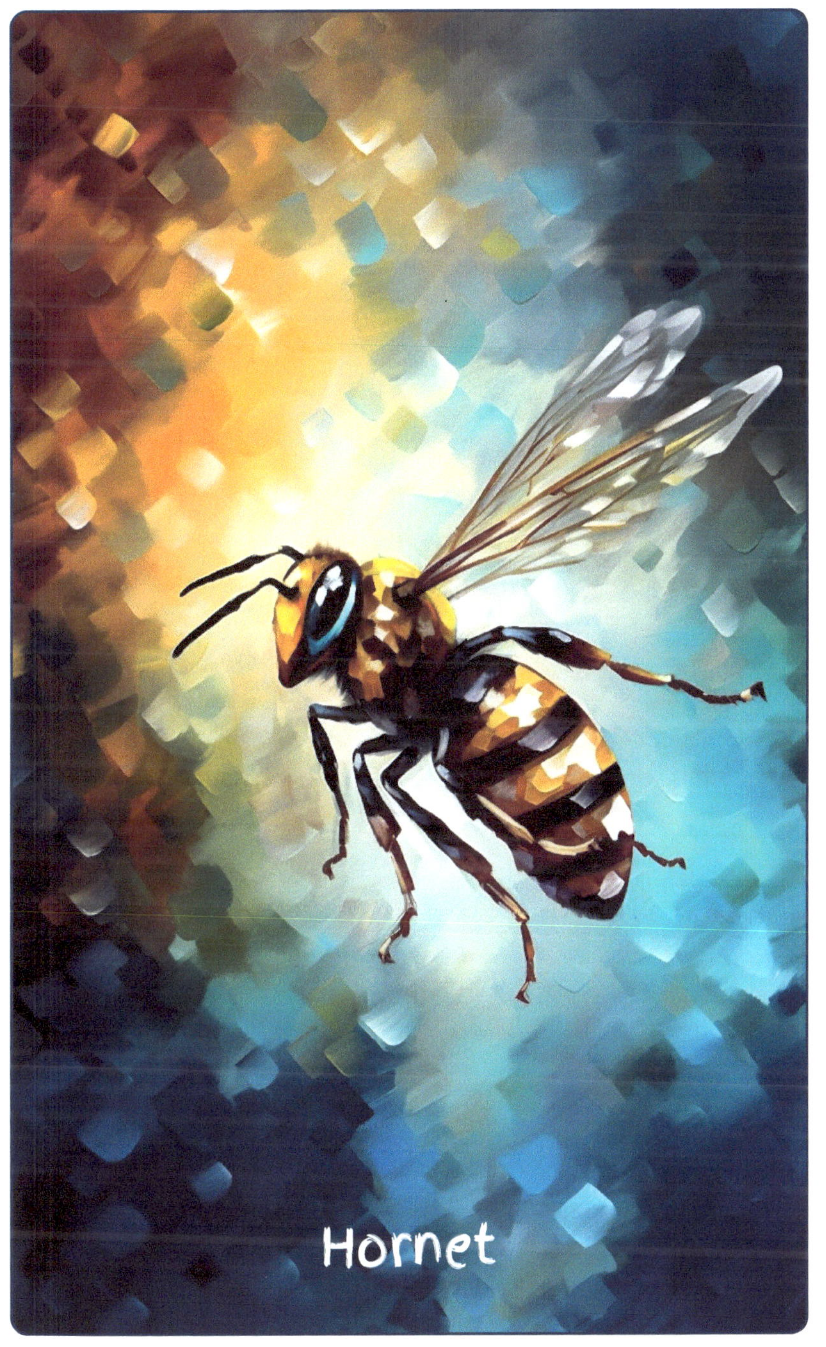

Hornet

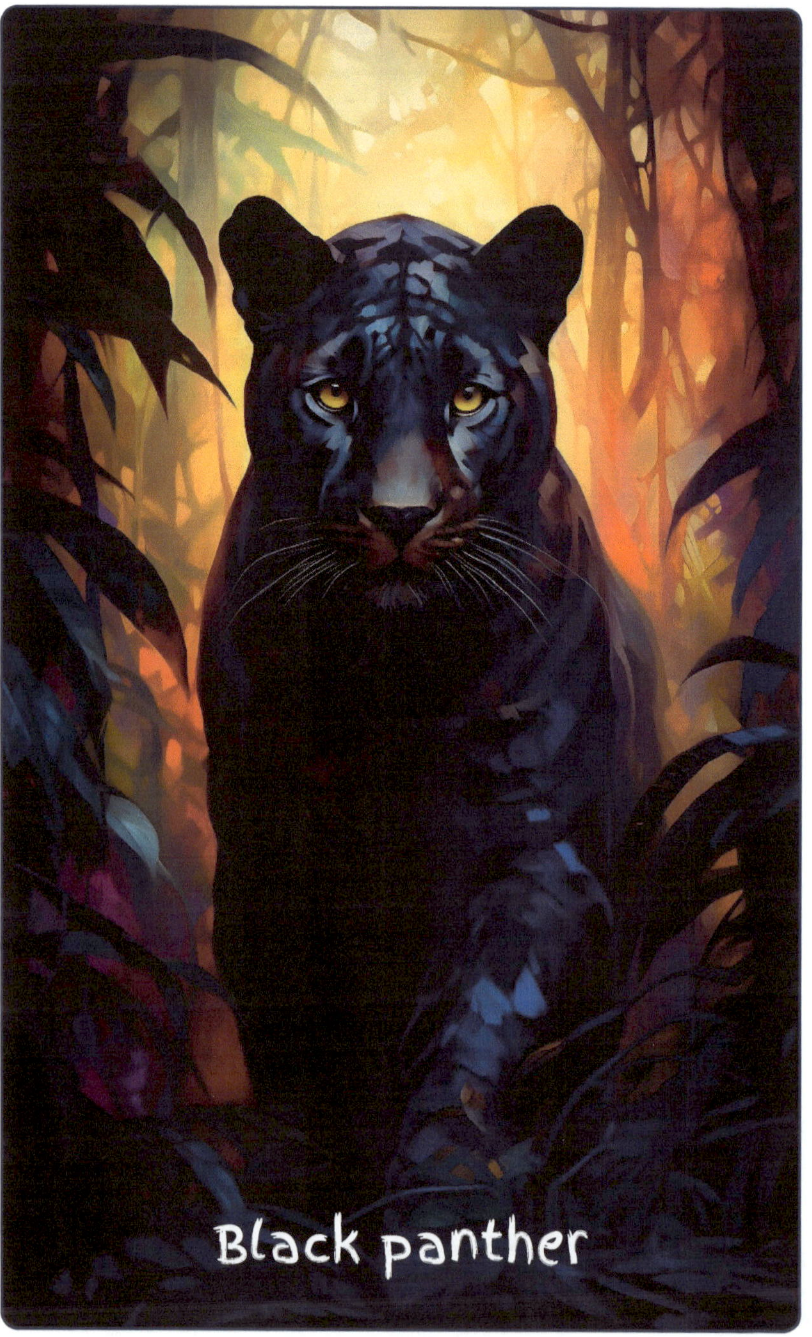

Black panther

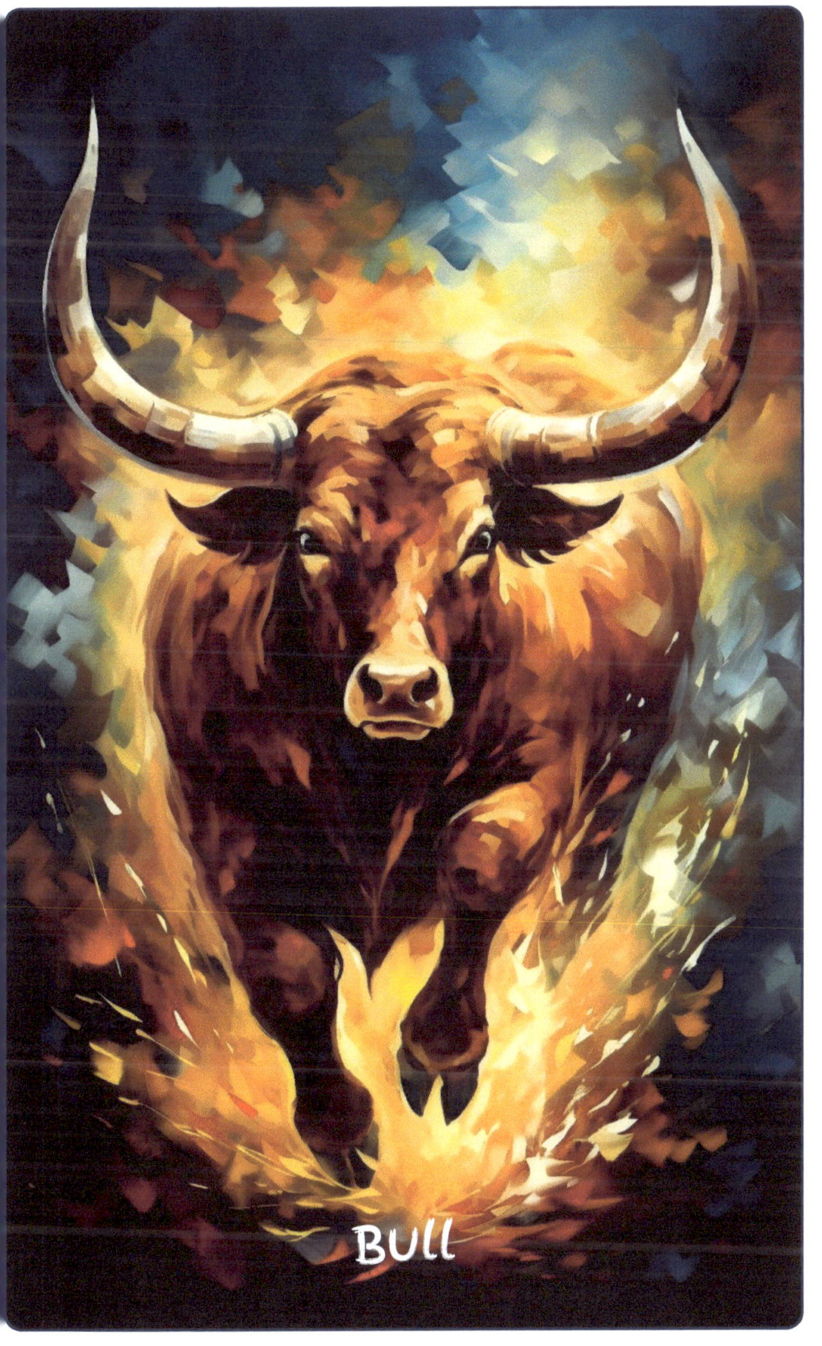

Bull

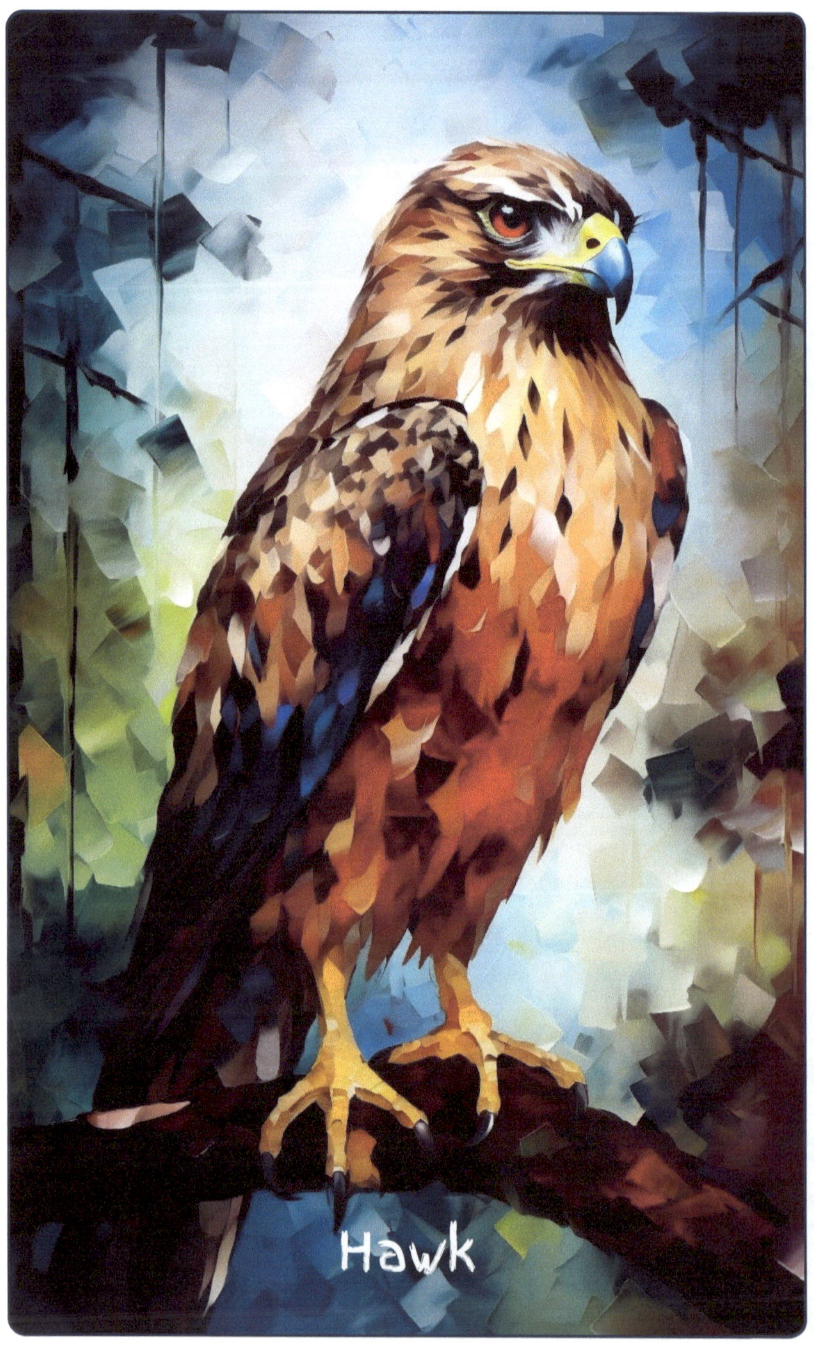

Hawk

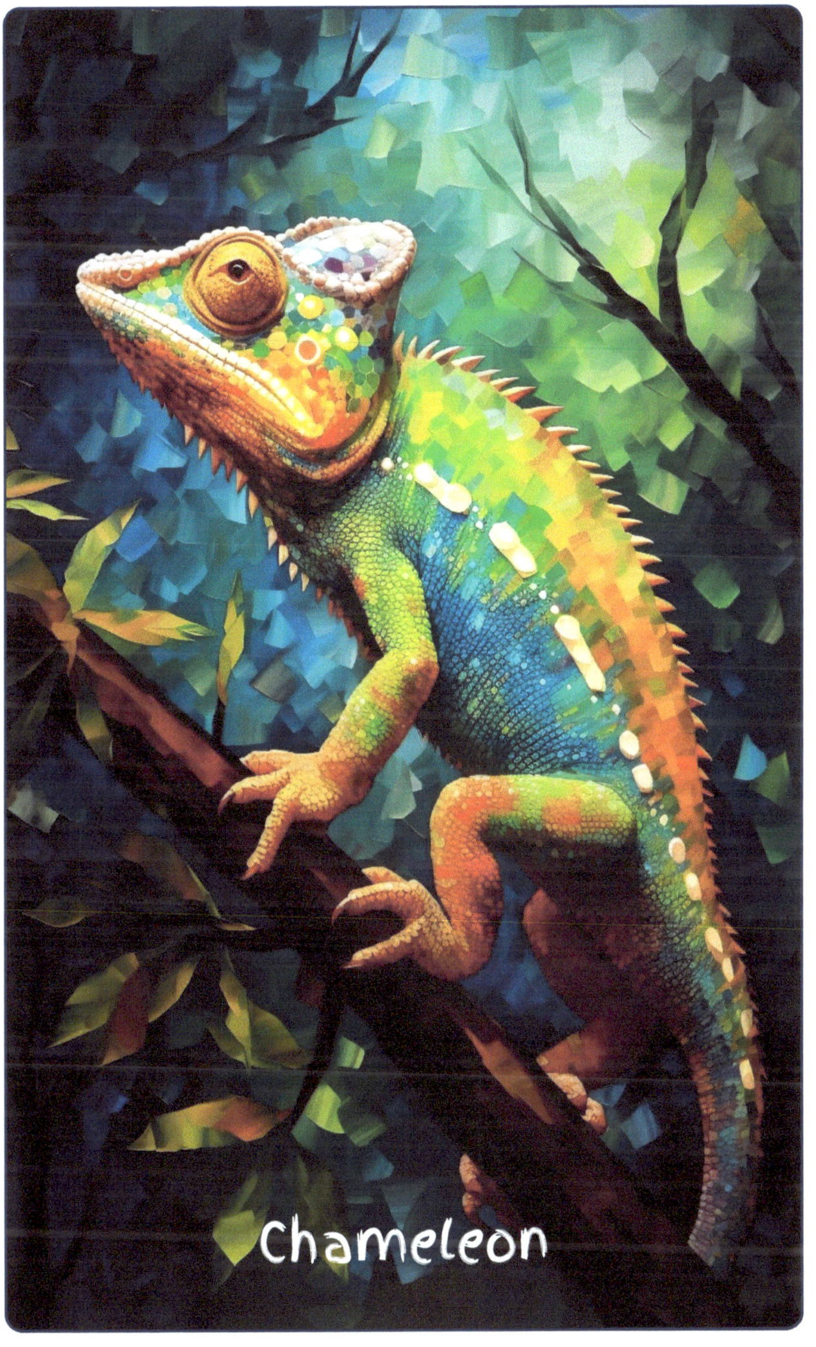

Chameleon

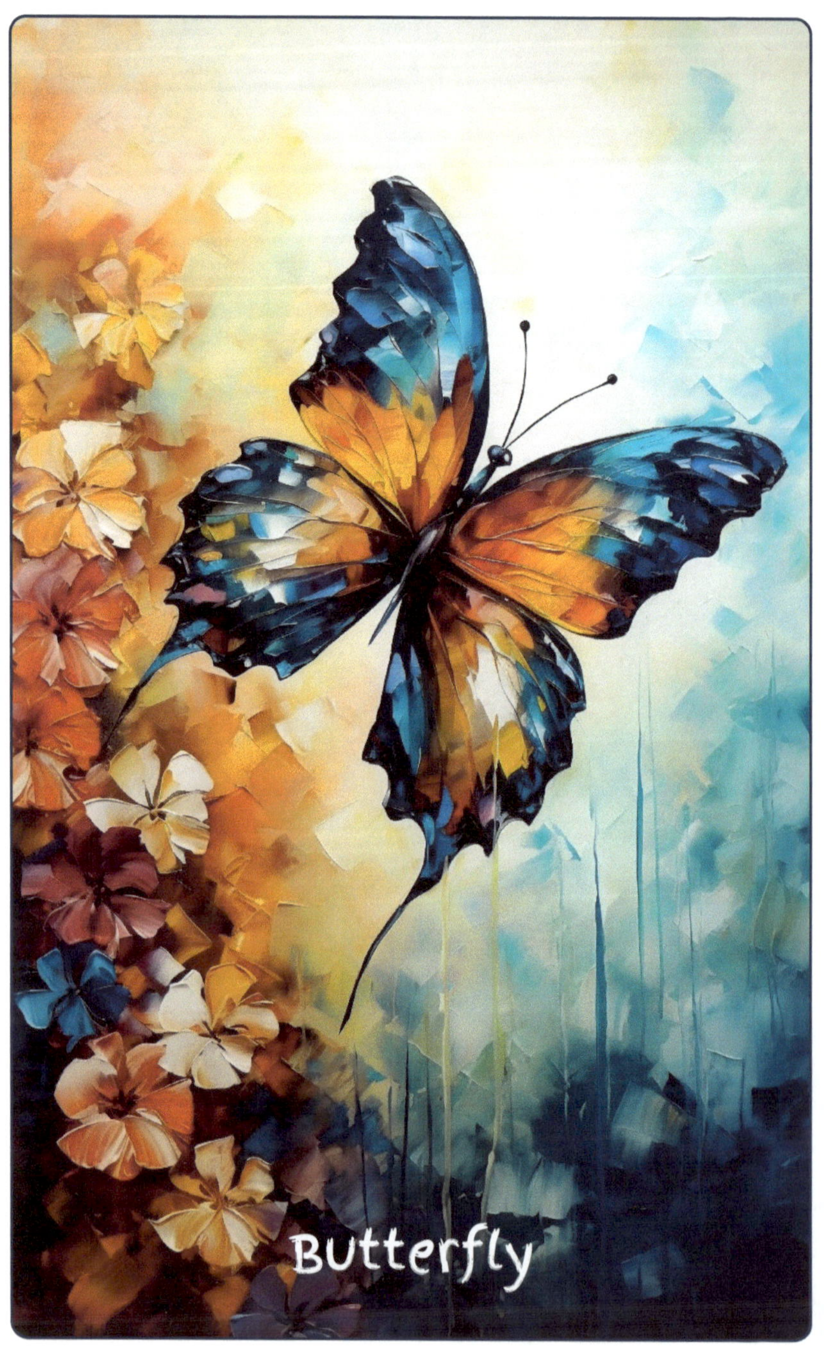

Butterfly

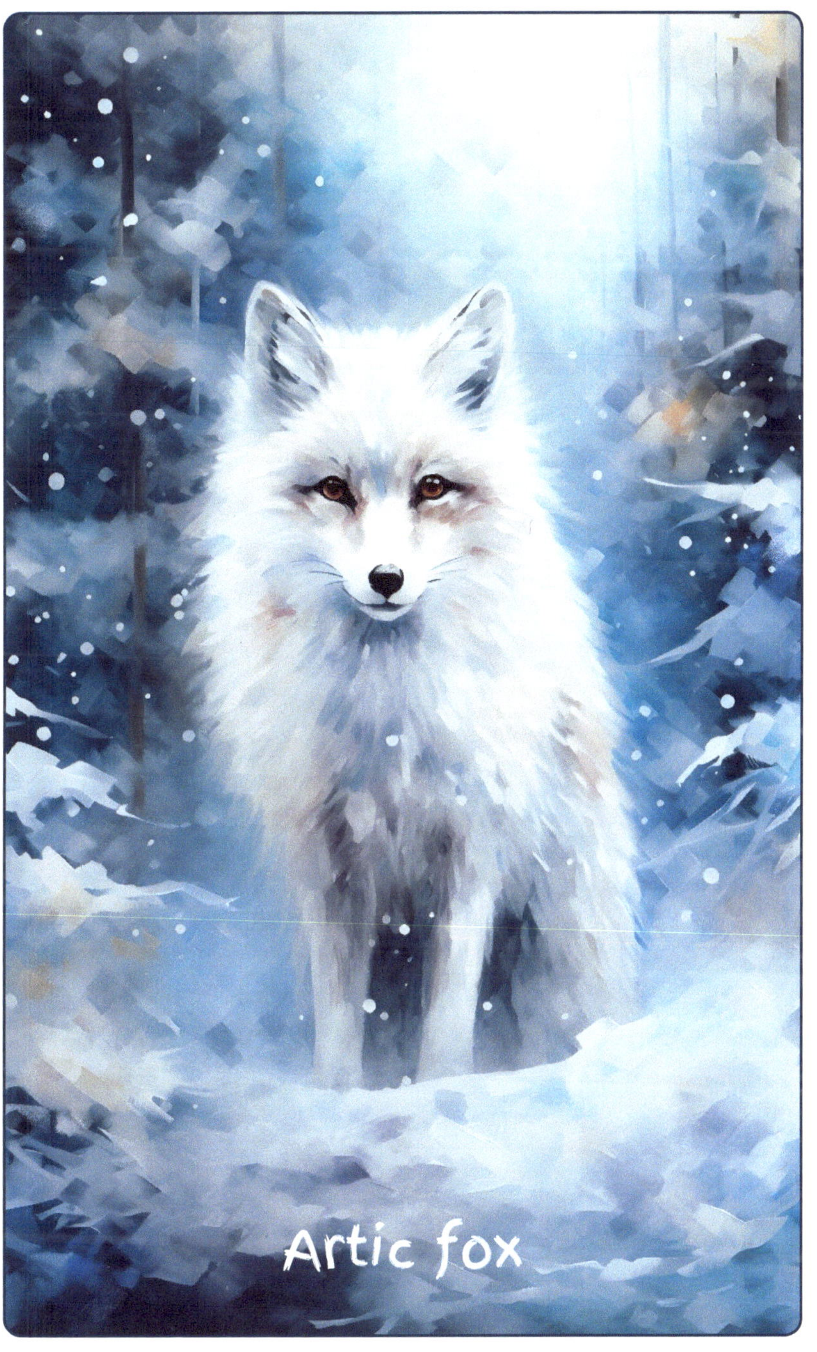

Artic fox

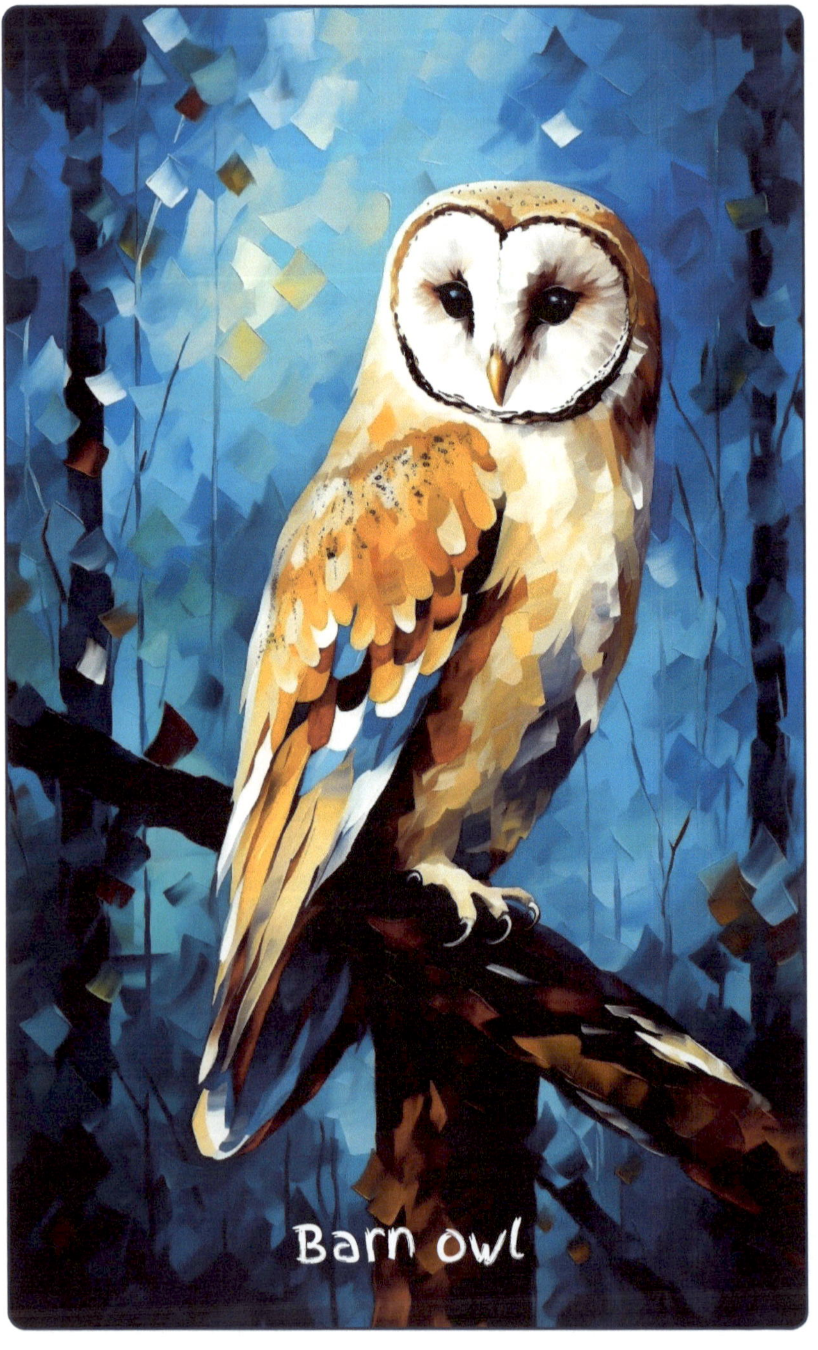
Barn owl

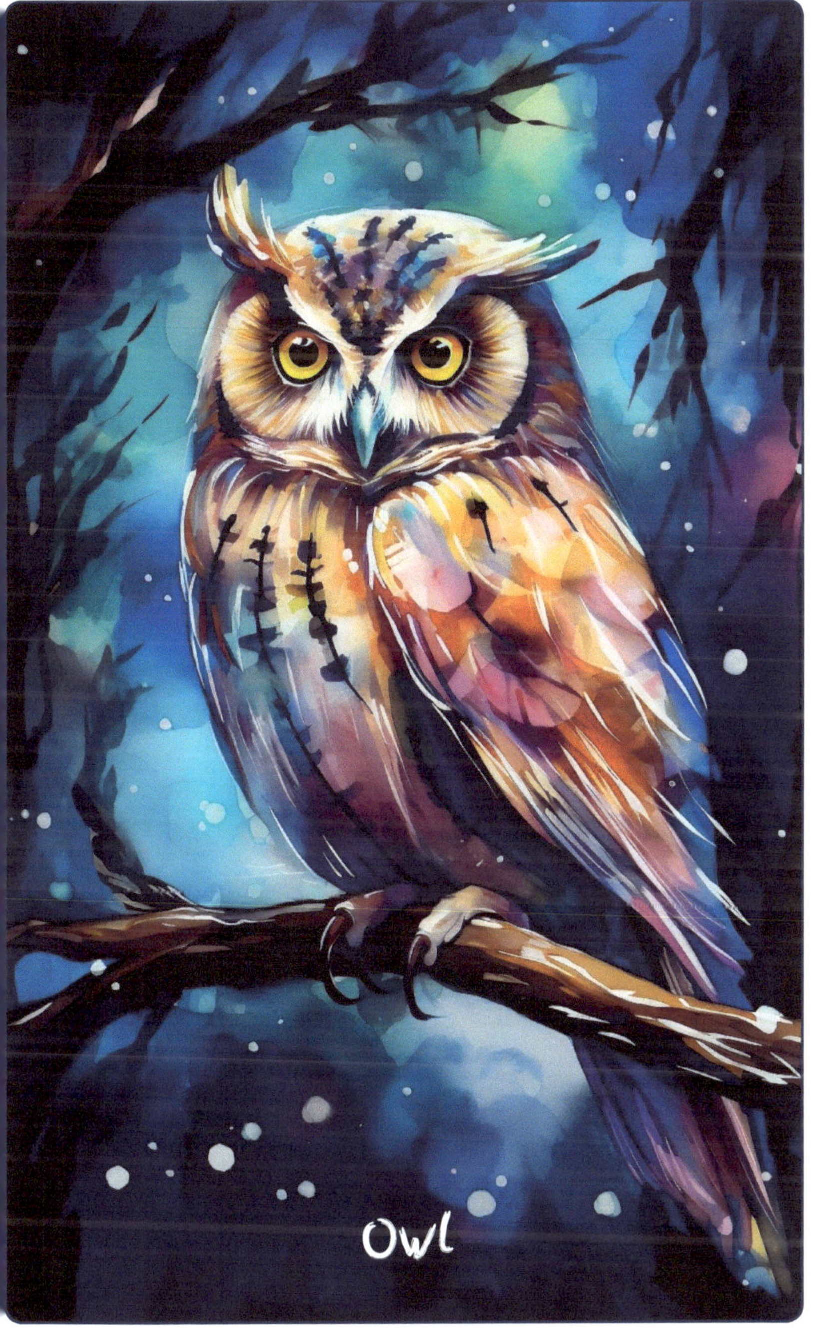

Owl

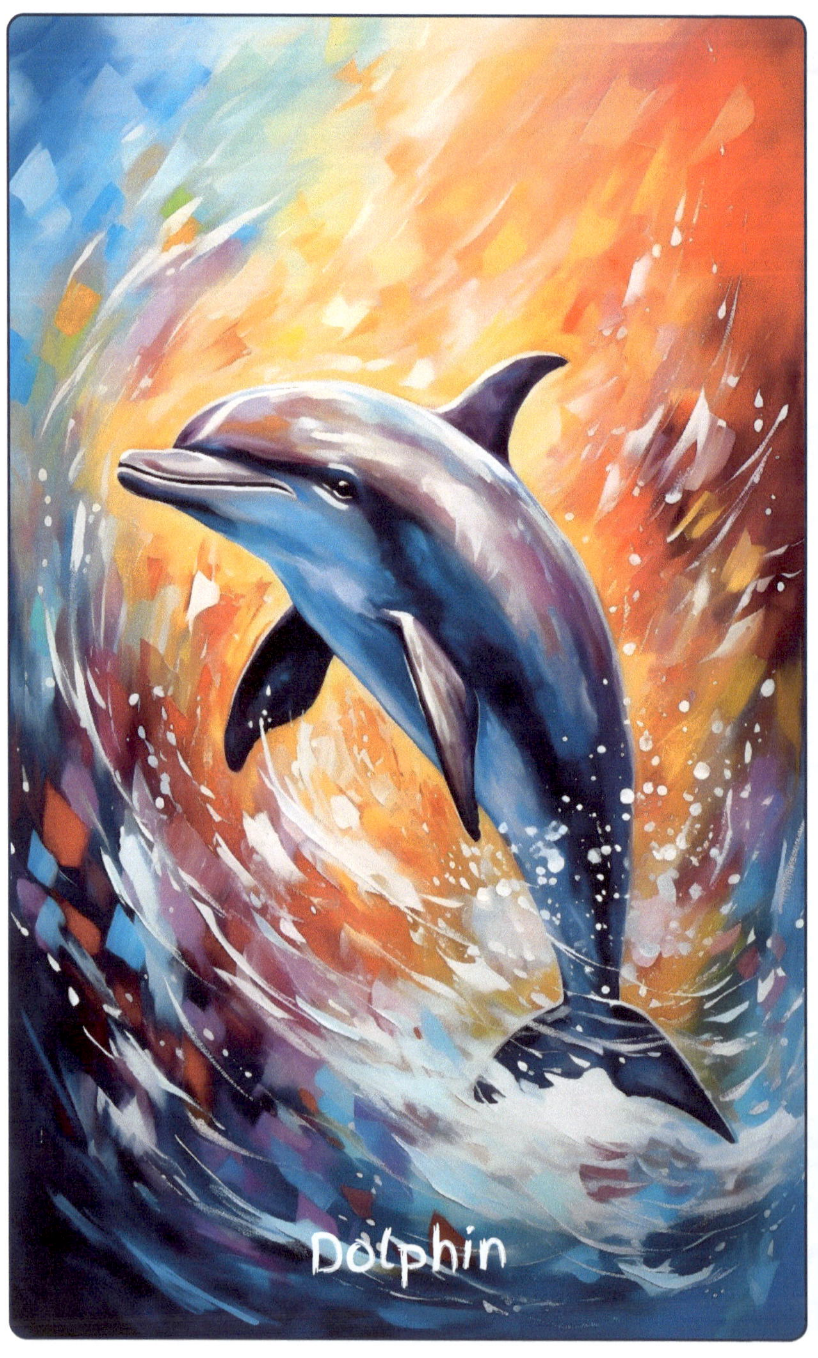
Dolphin

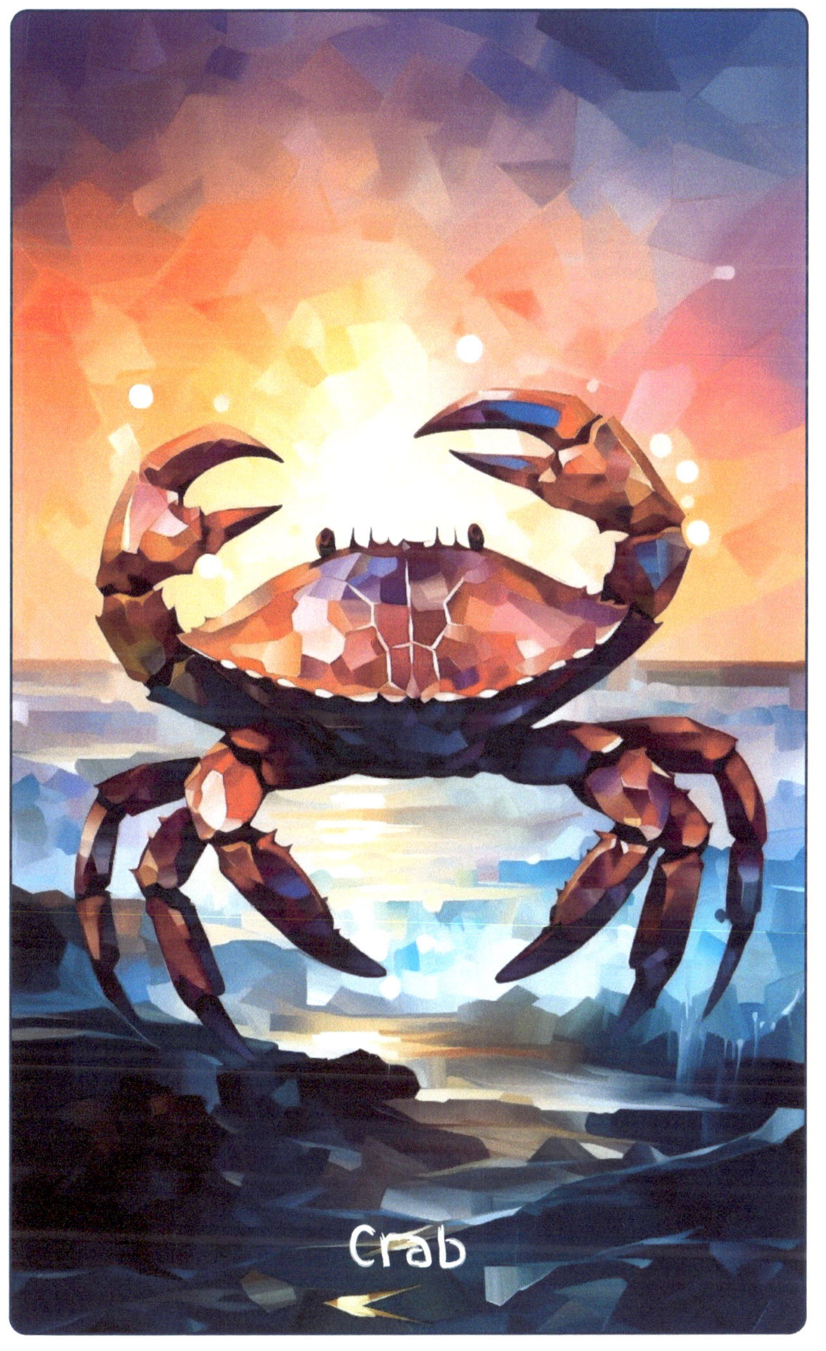

Crab

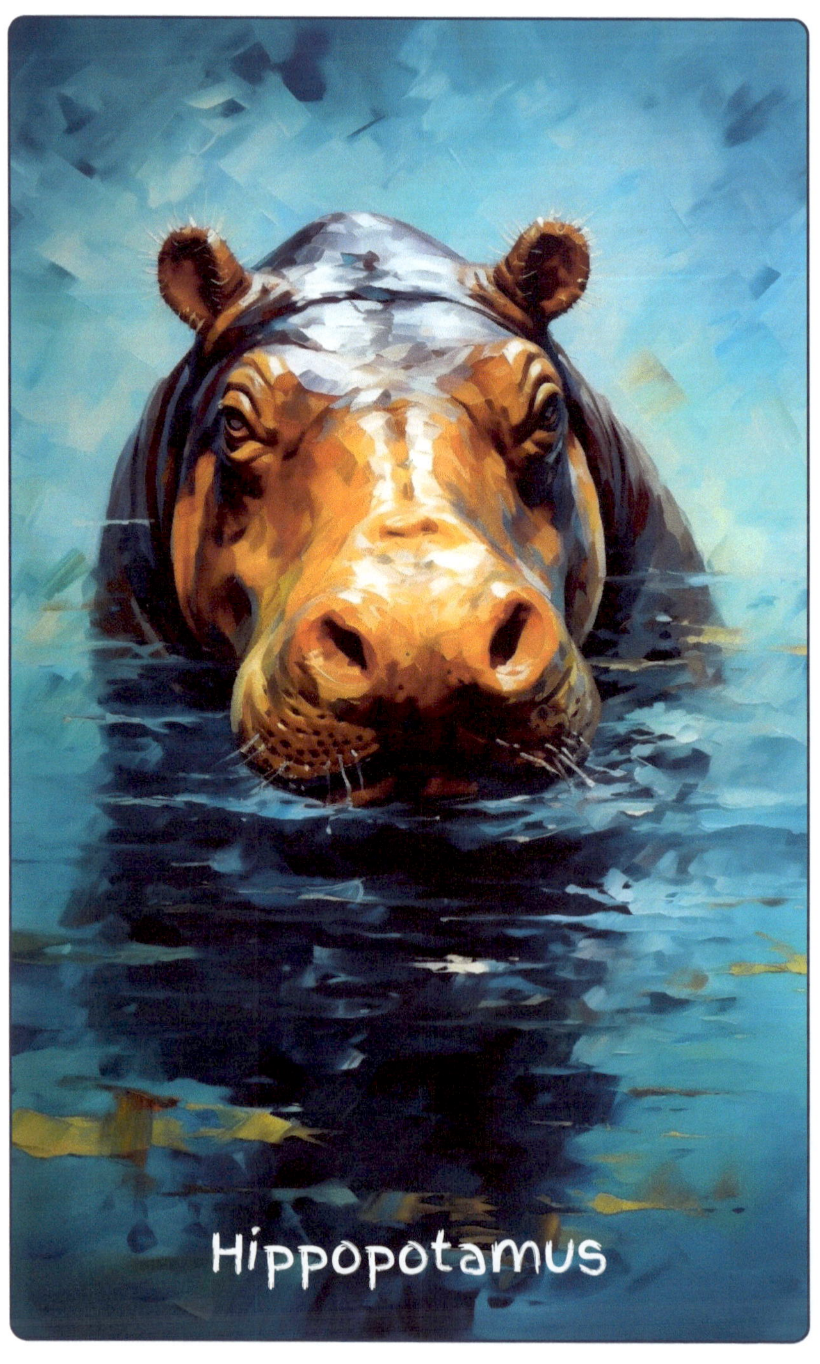

Hippopotamus

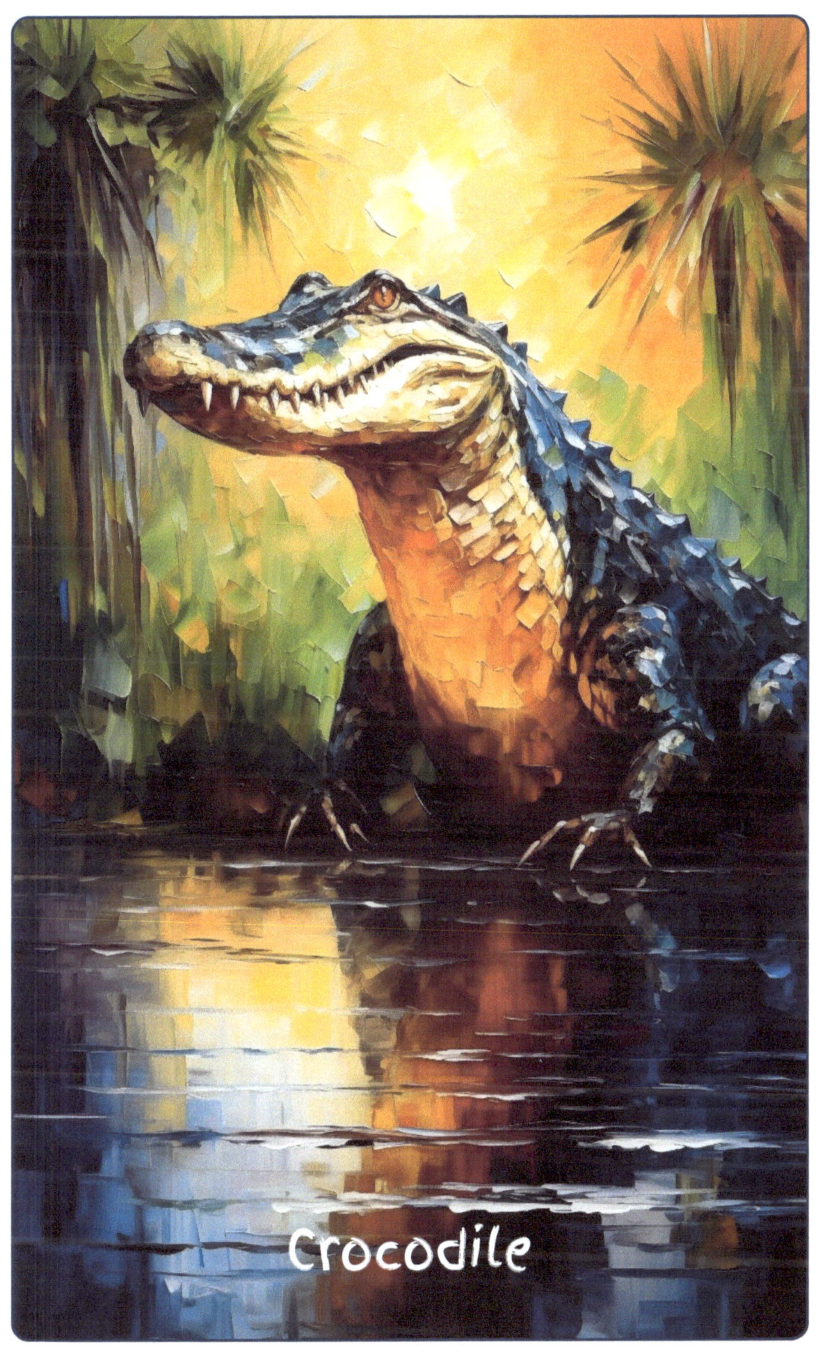

Crocodile

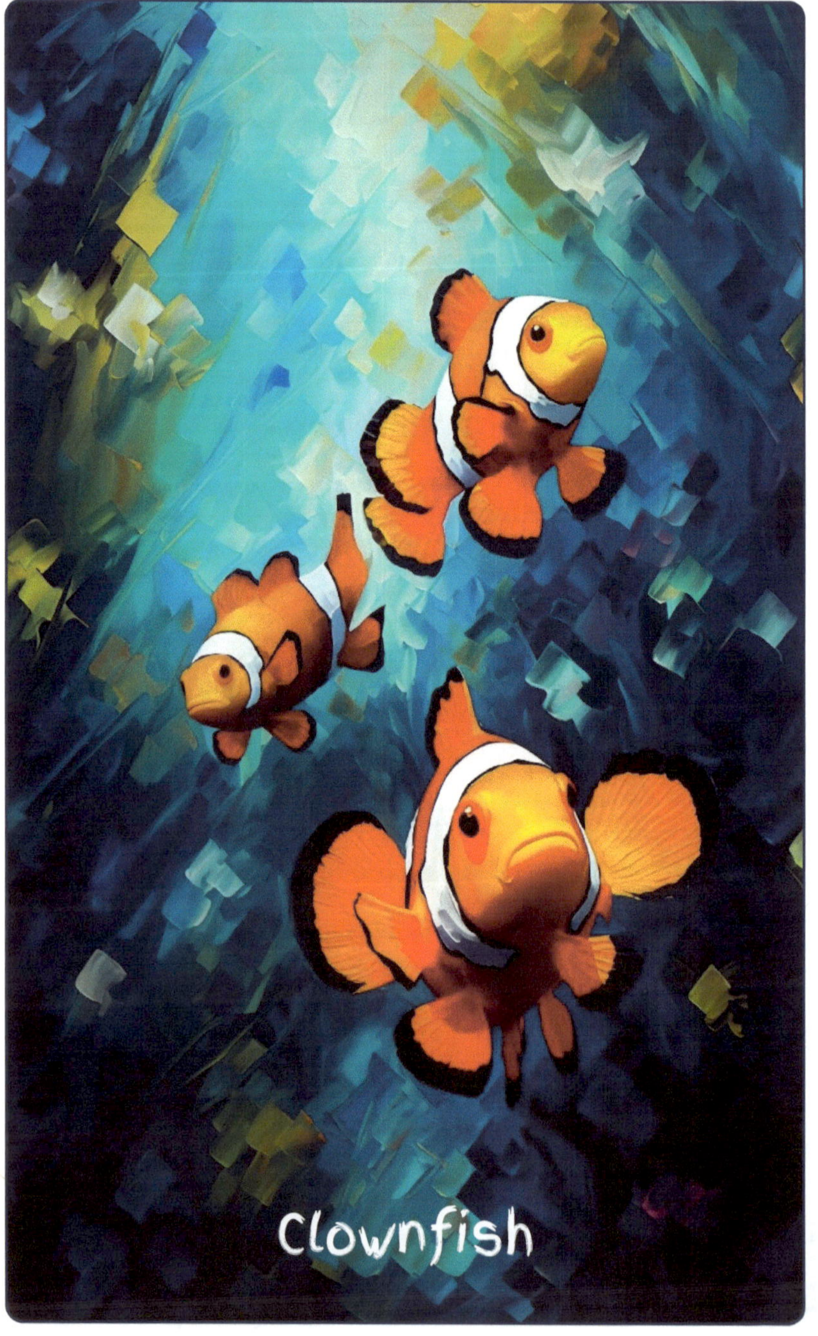

Clownfish

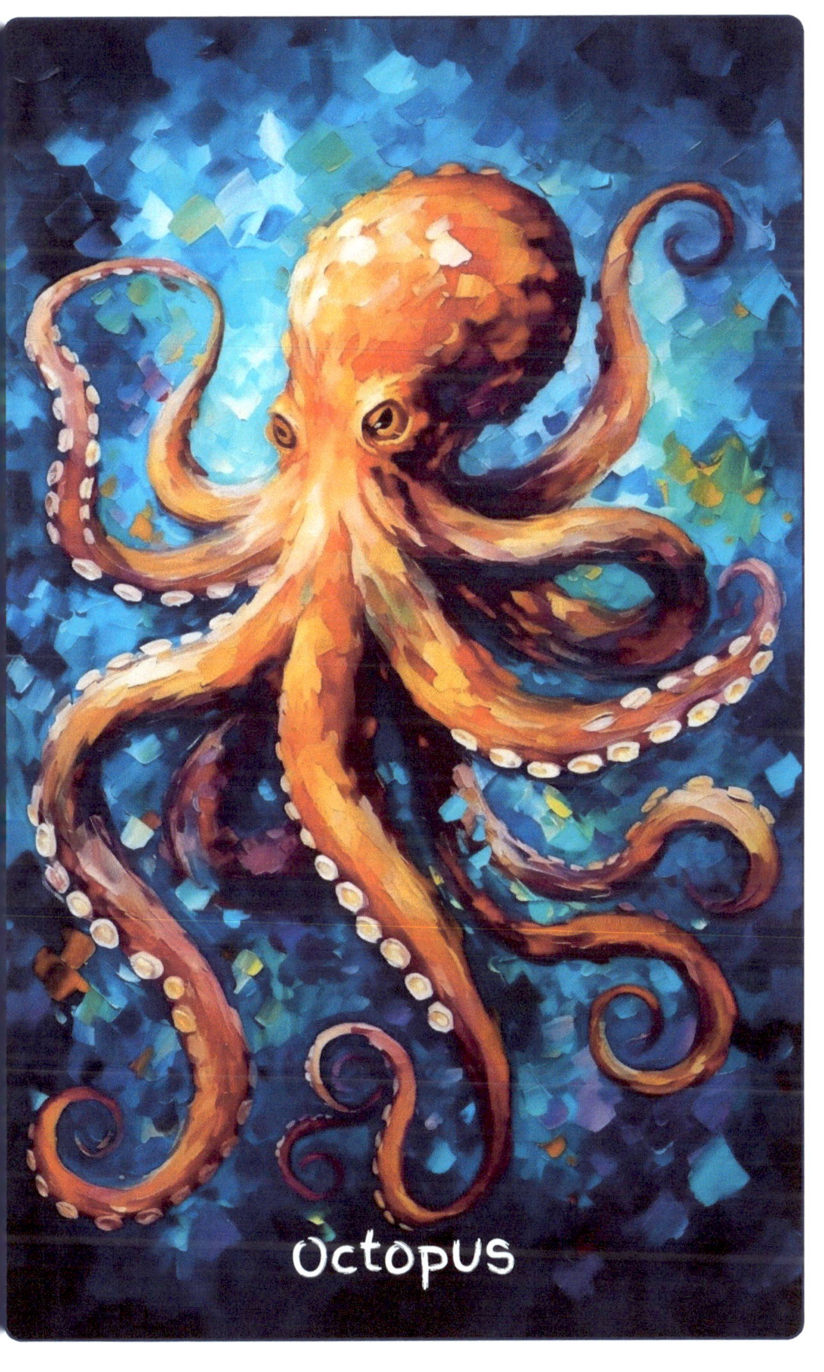

Octopus

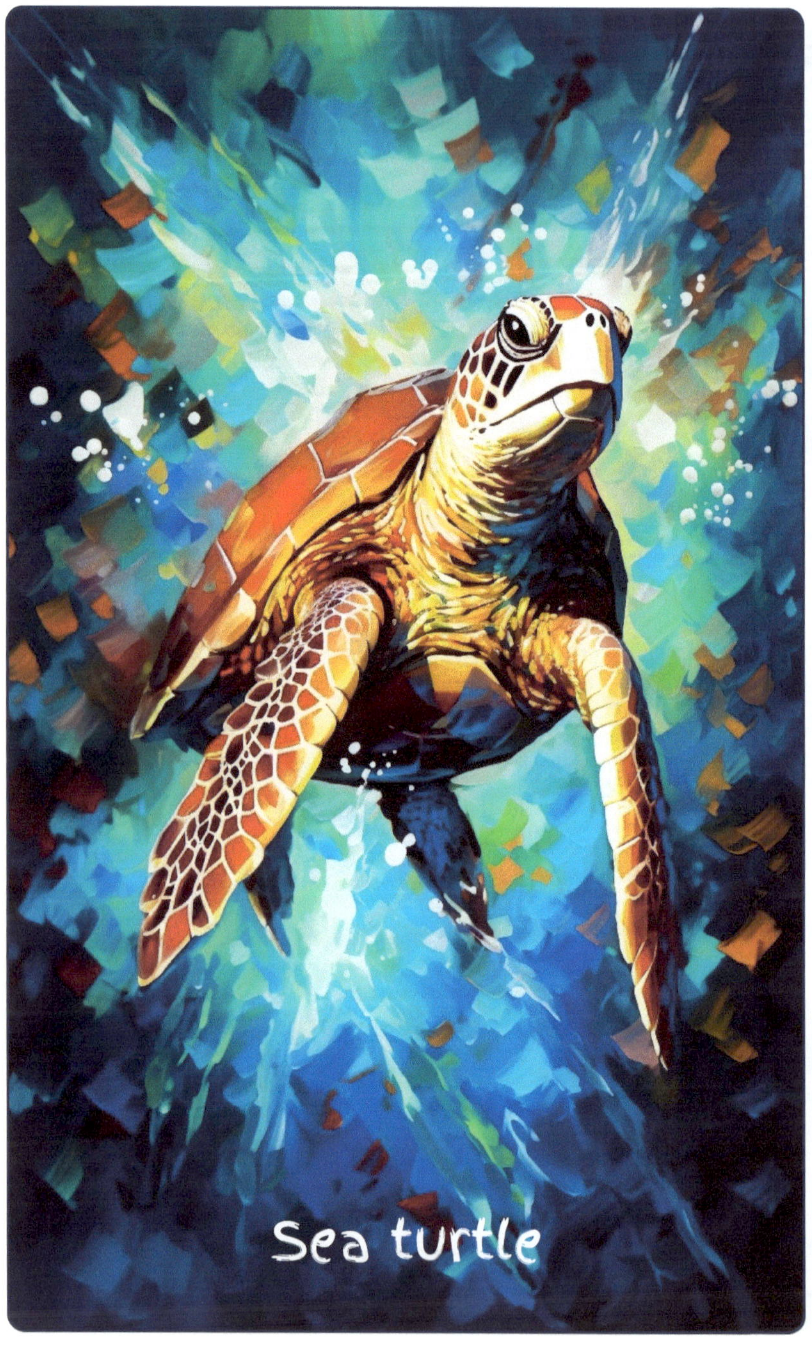

Sea turtle

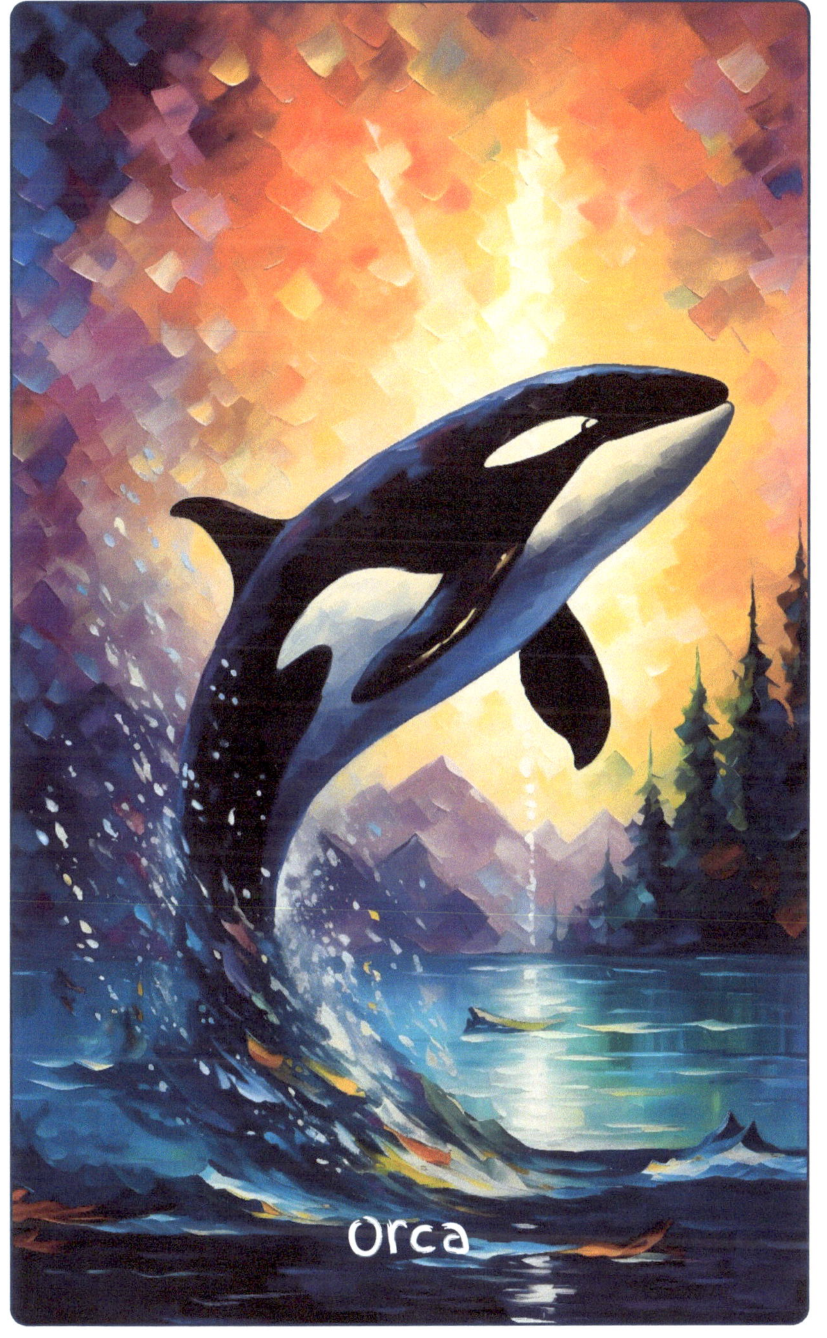
Orca

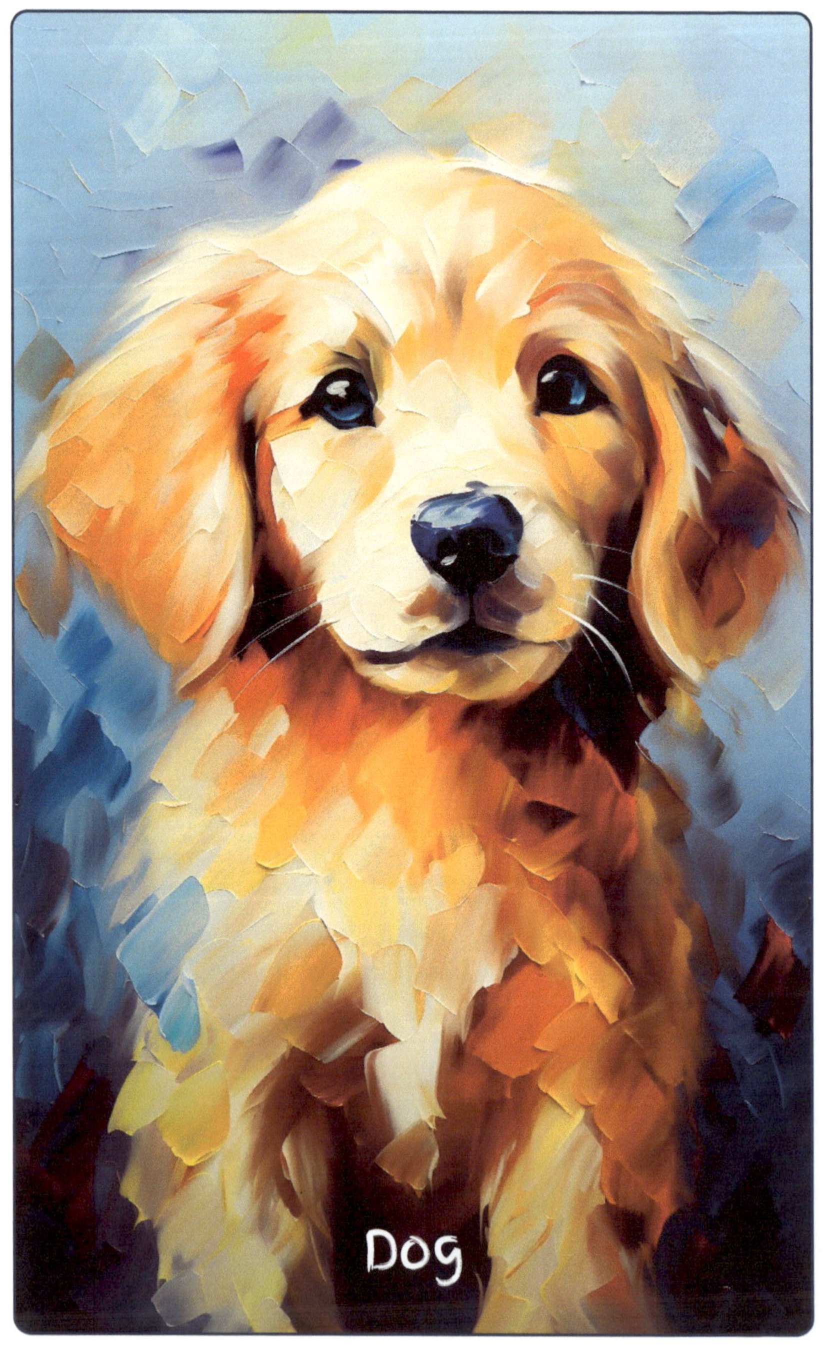
Dog

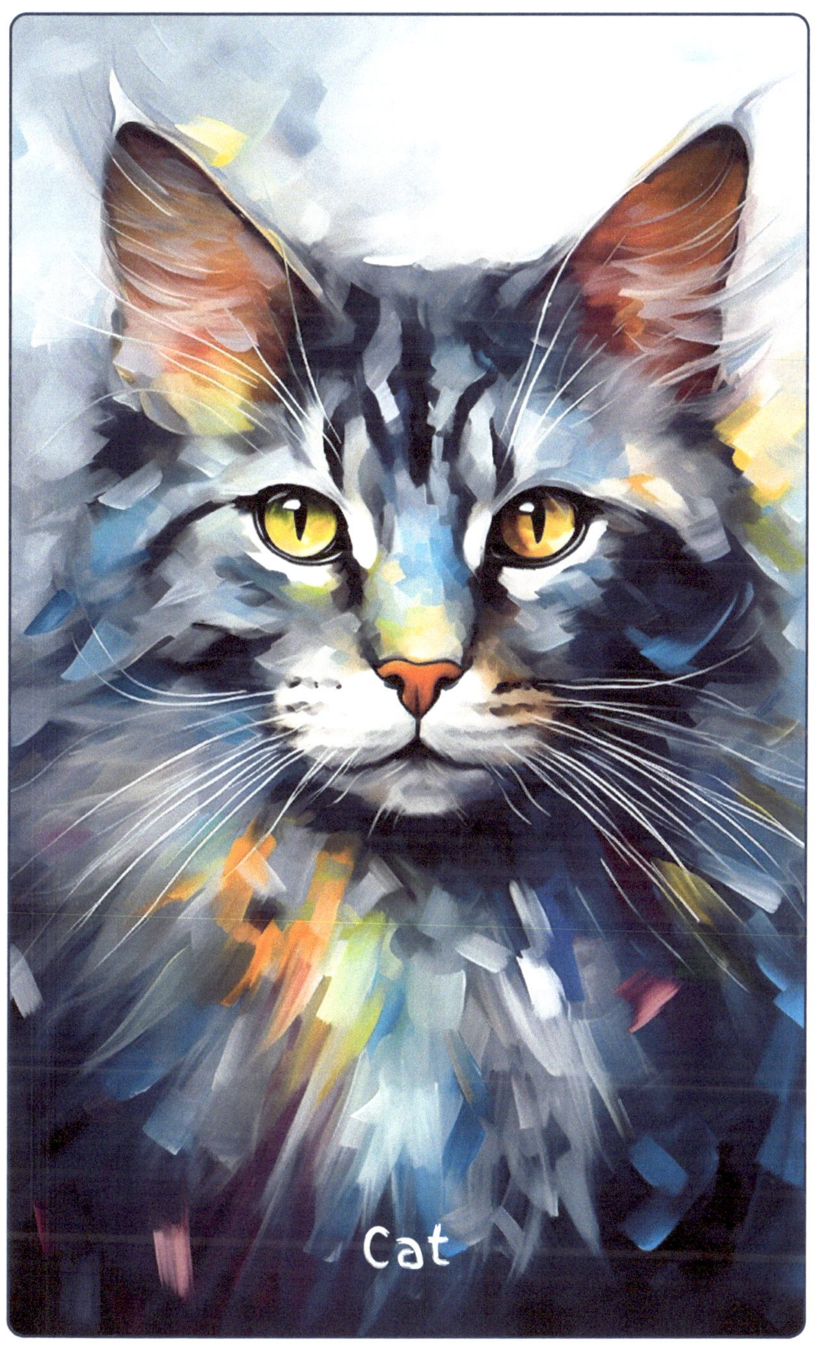
Cat

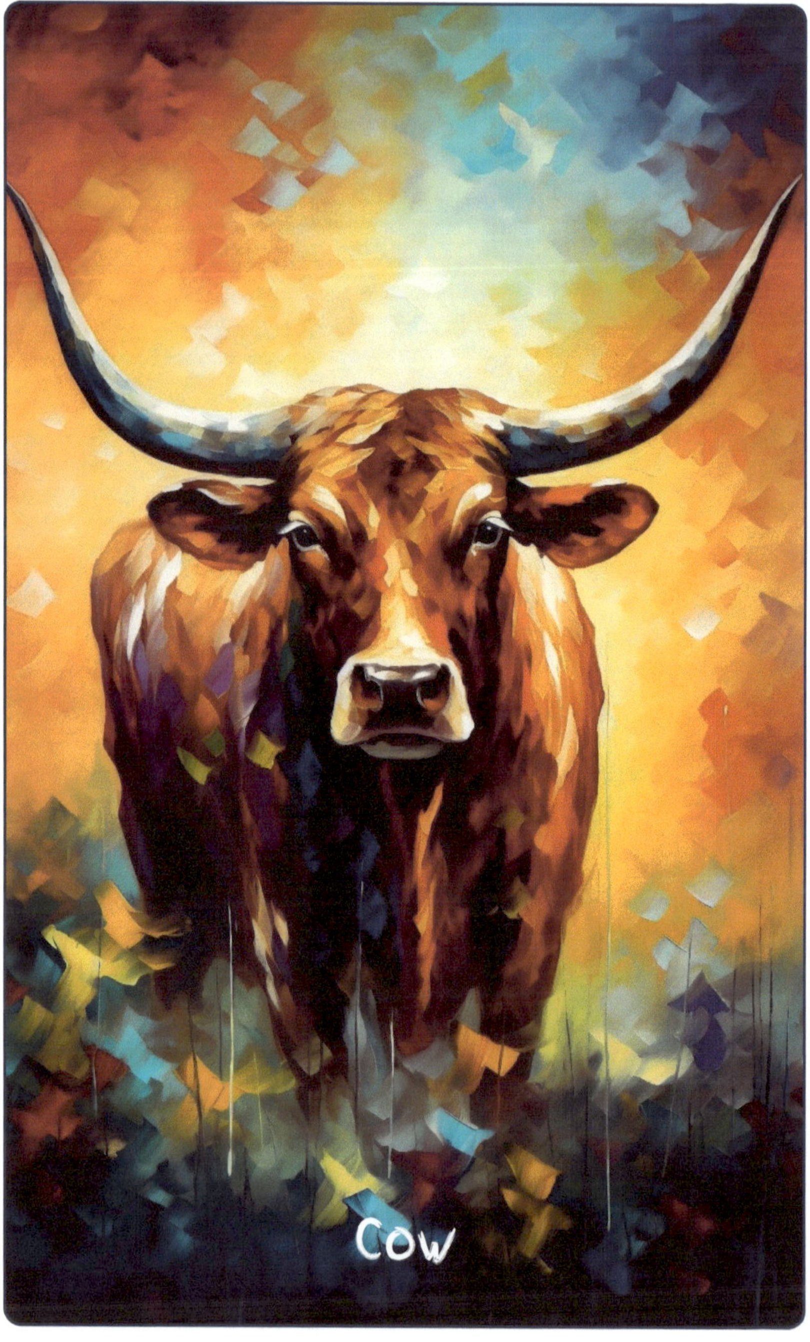

Cow

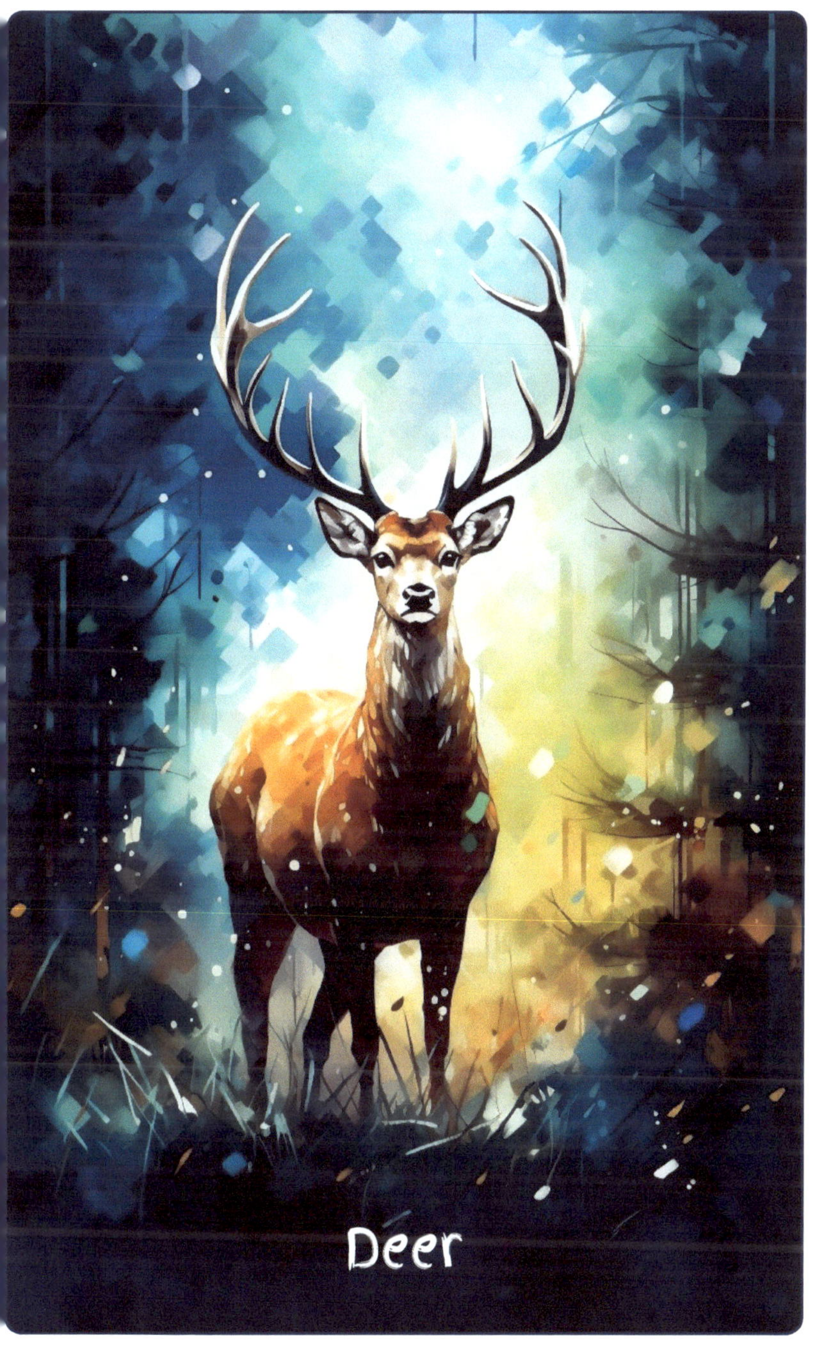

Deer

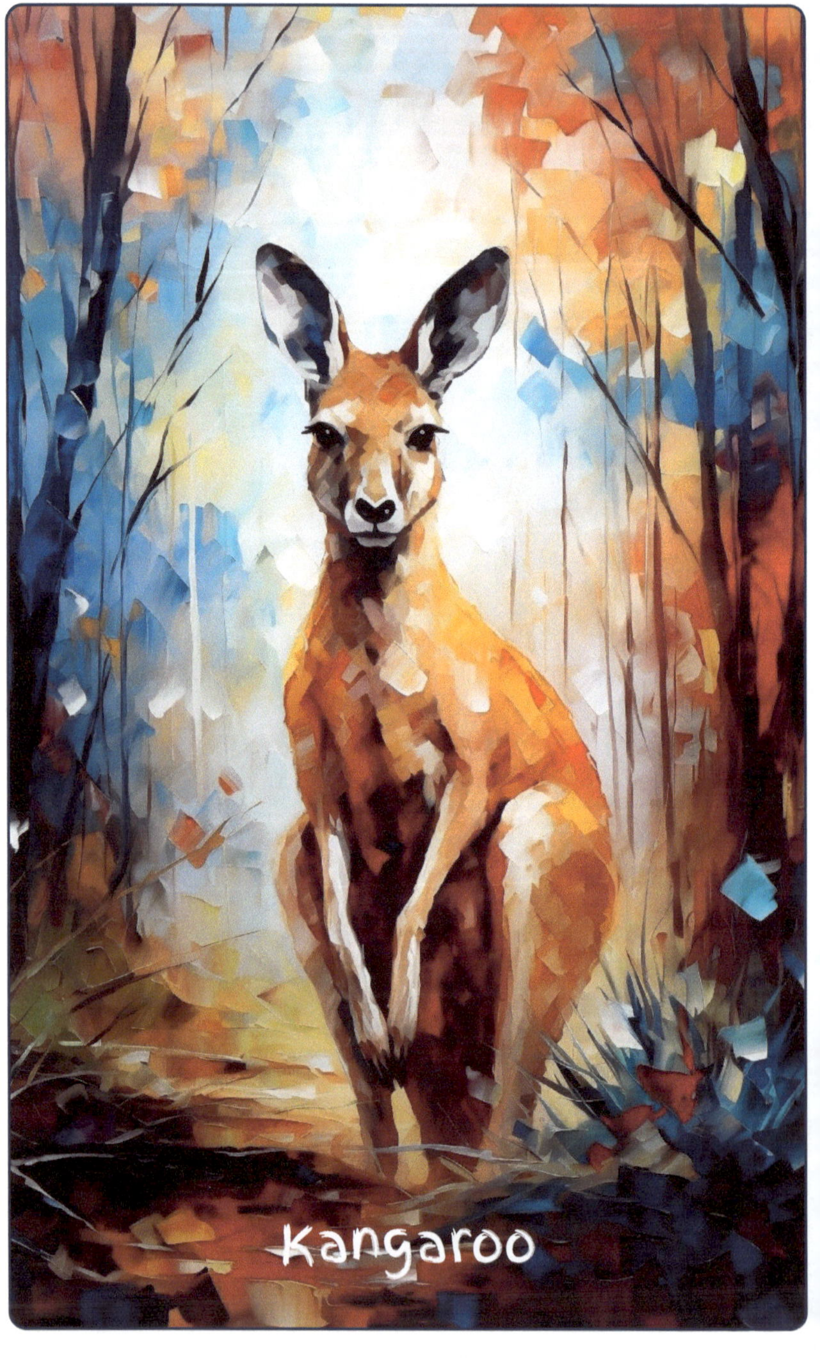
Kangaroo

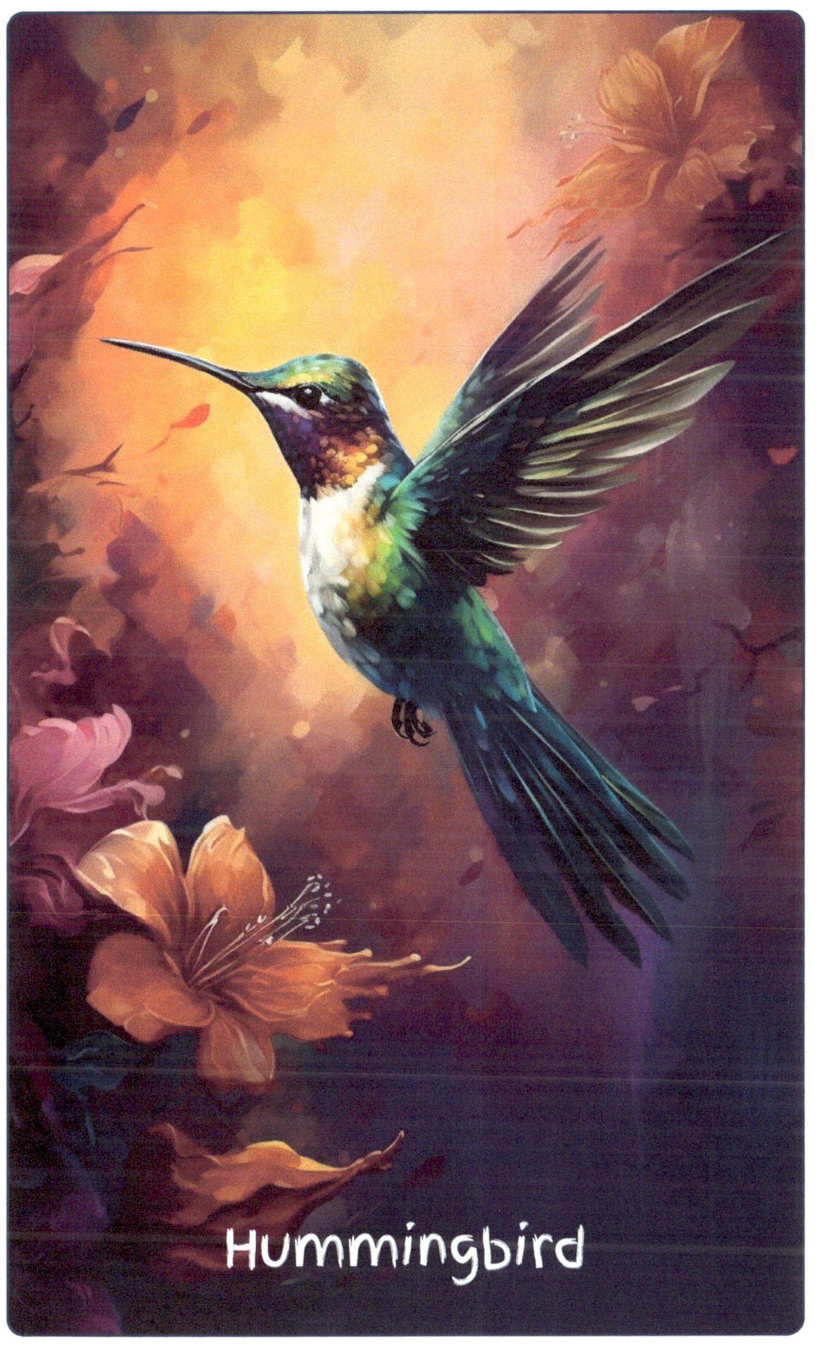

Hummingbird

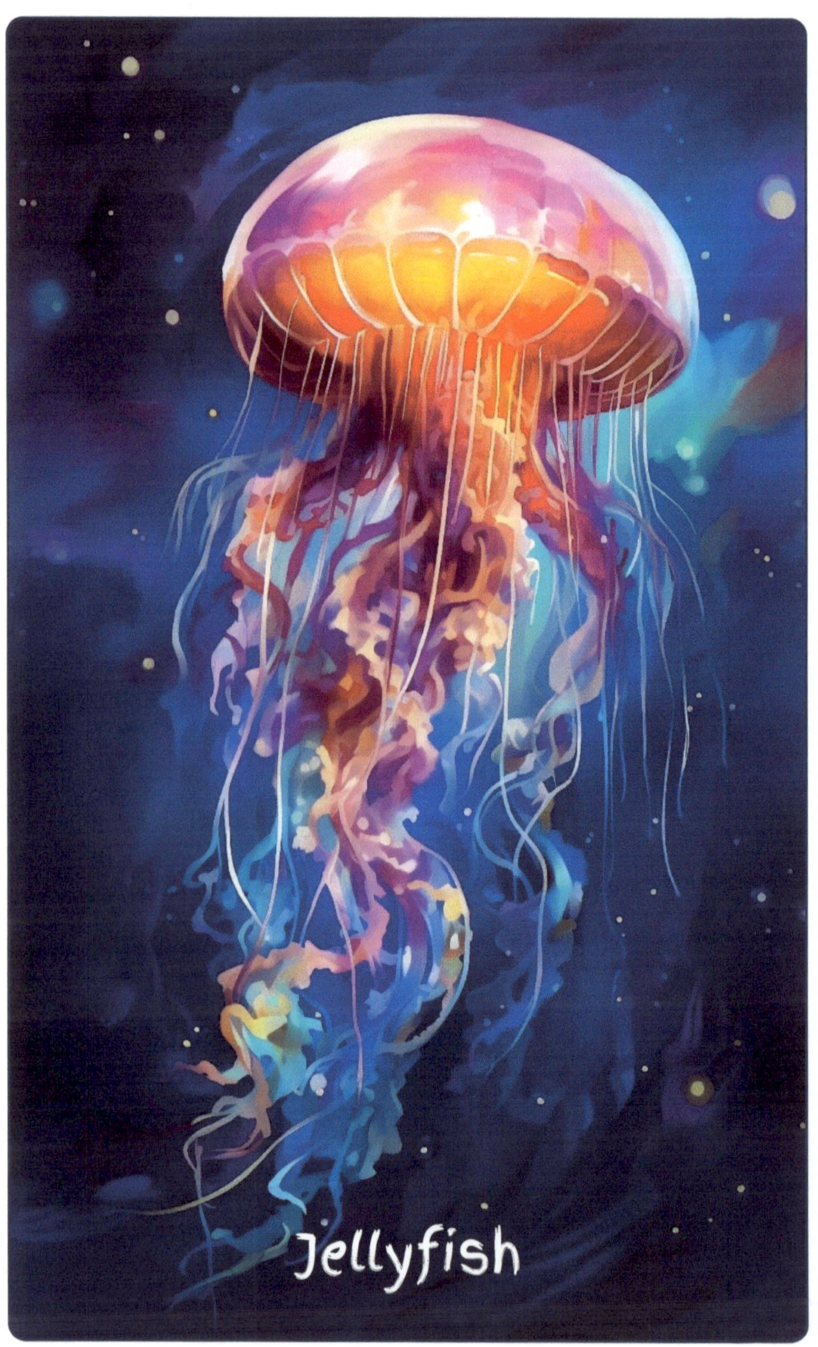

Jellyfish

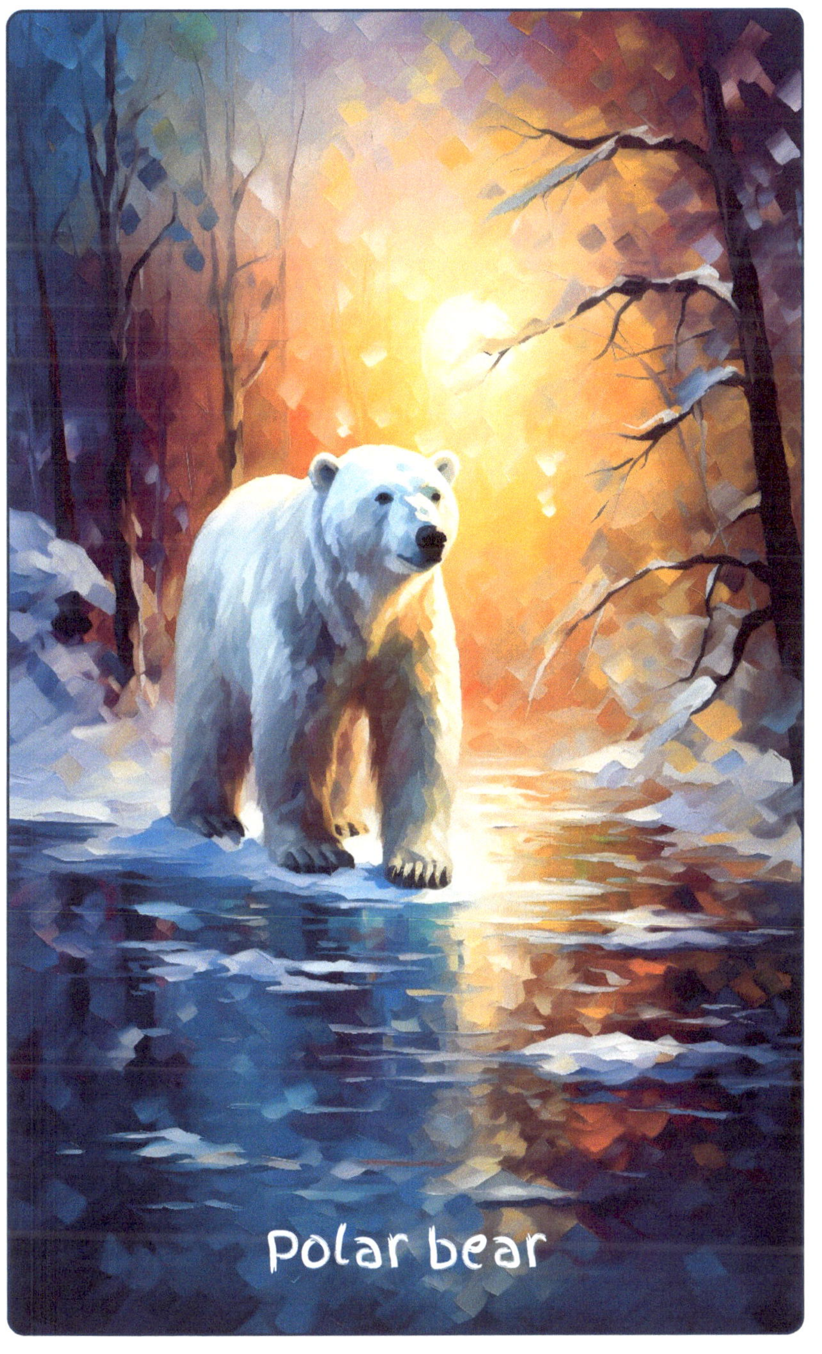

polar bear

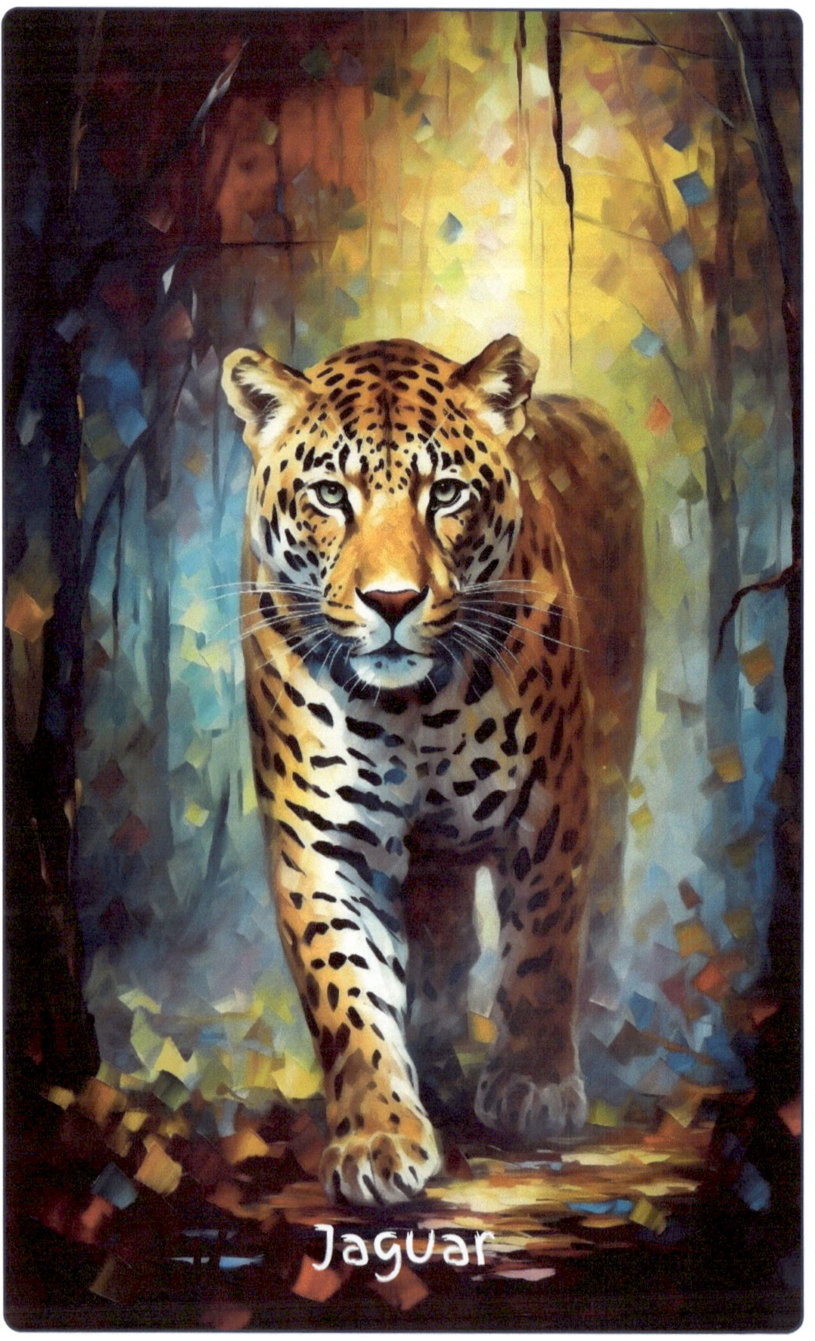
Jaguar

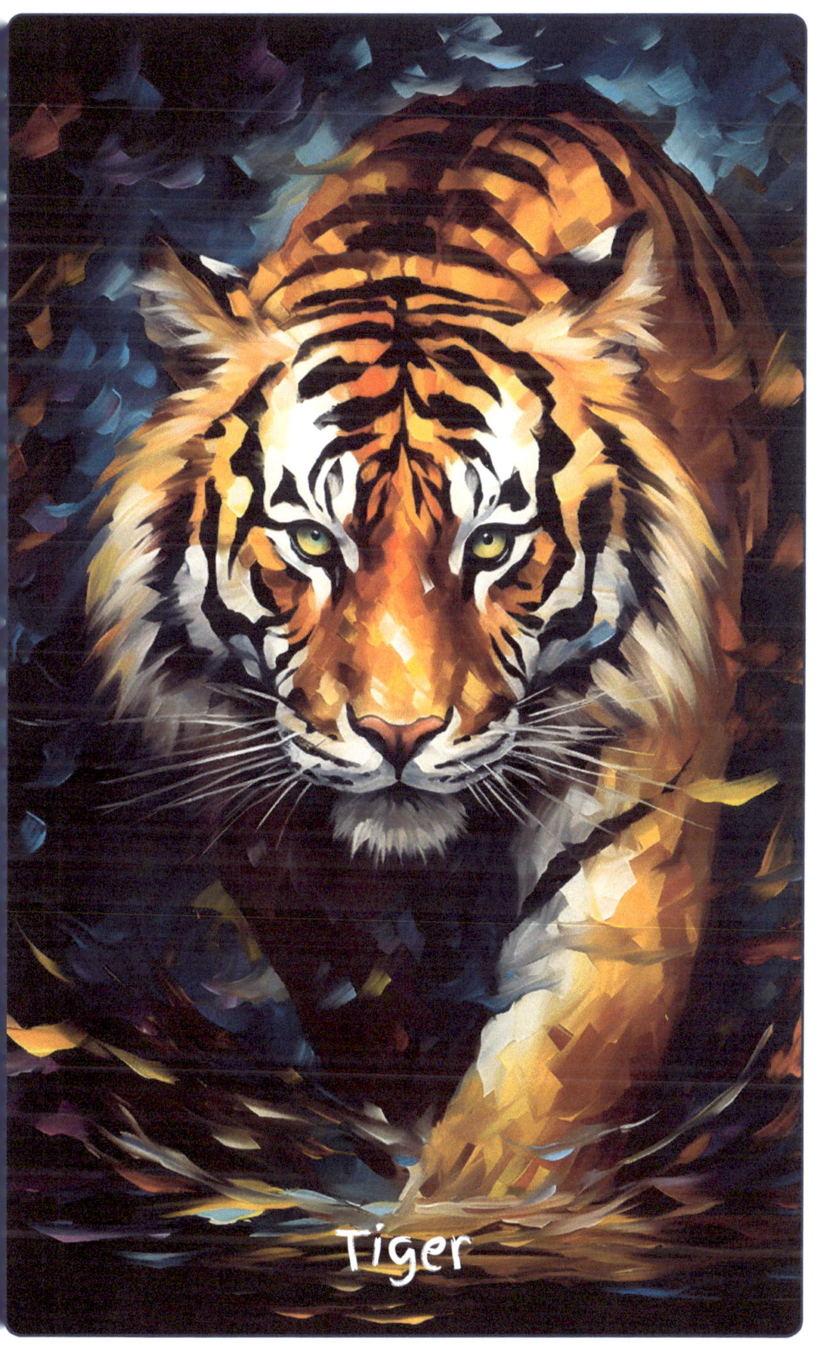

Tiger

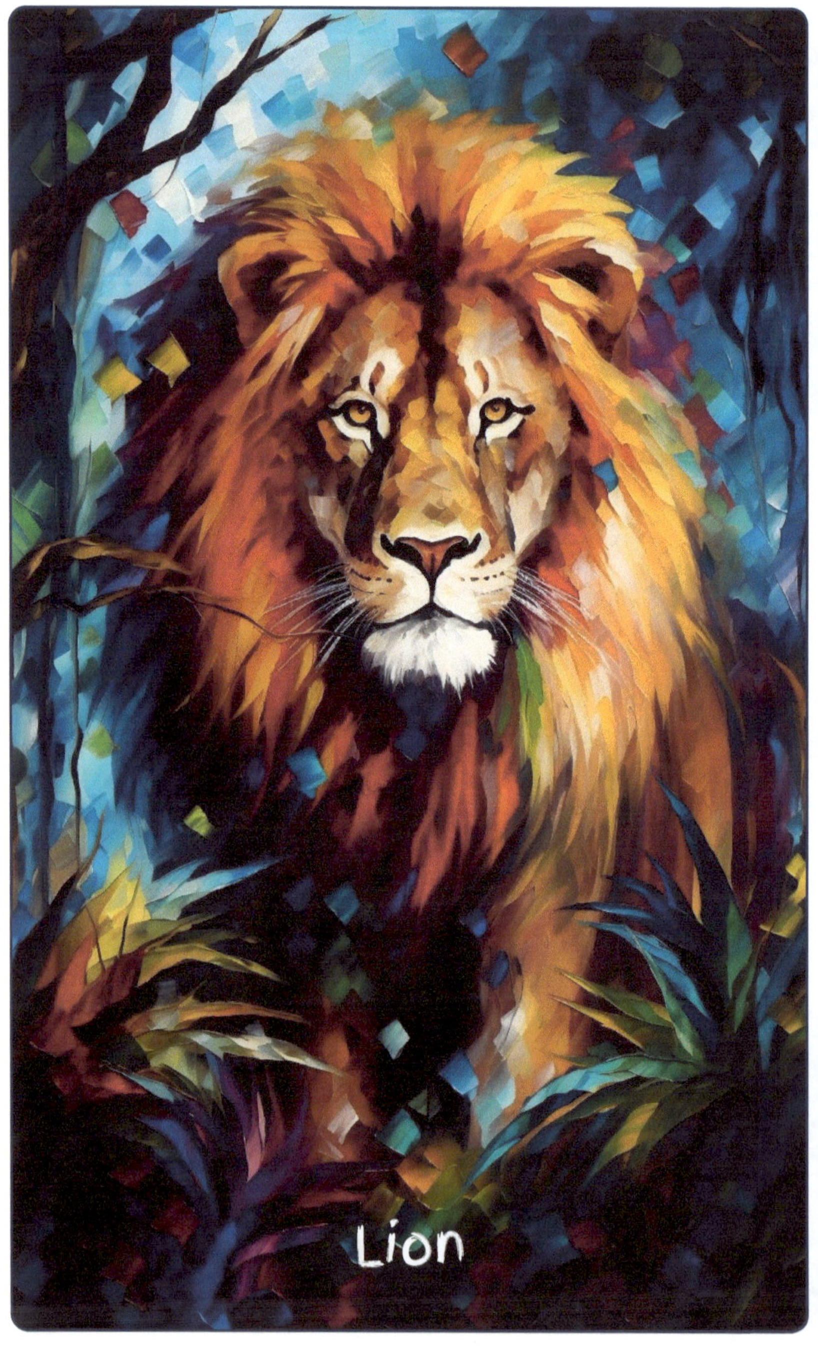
Lion

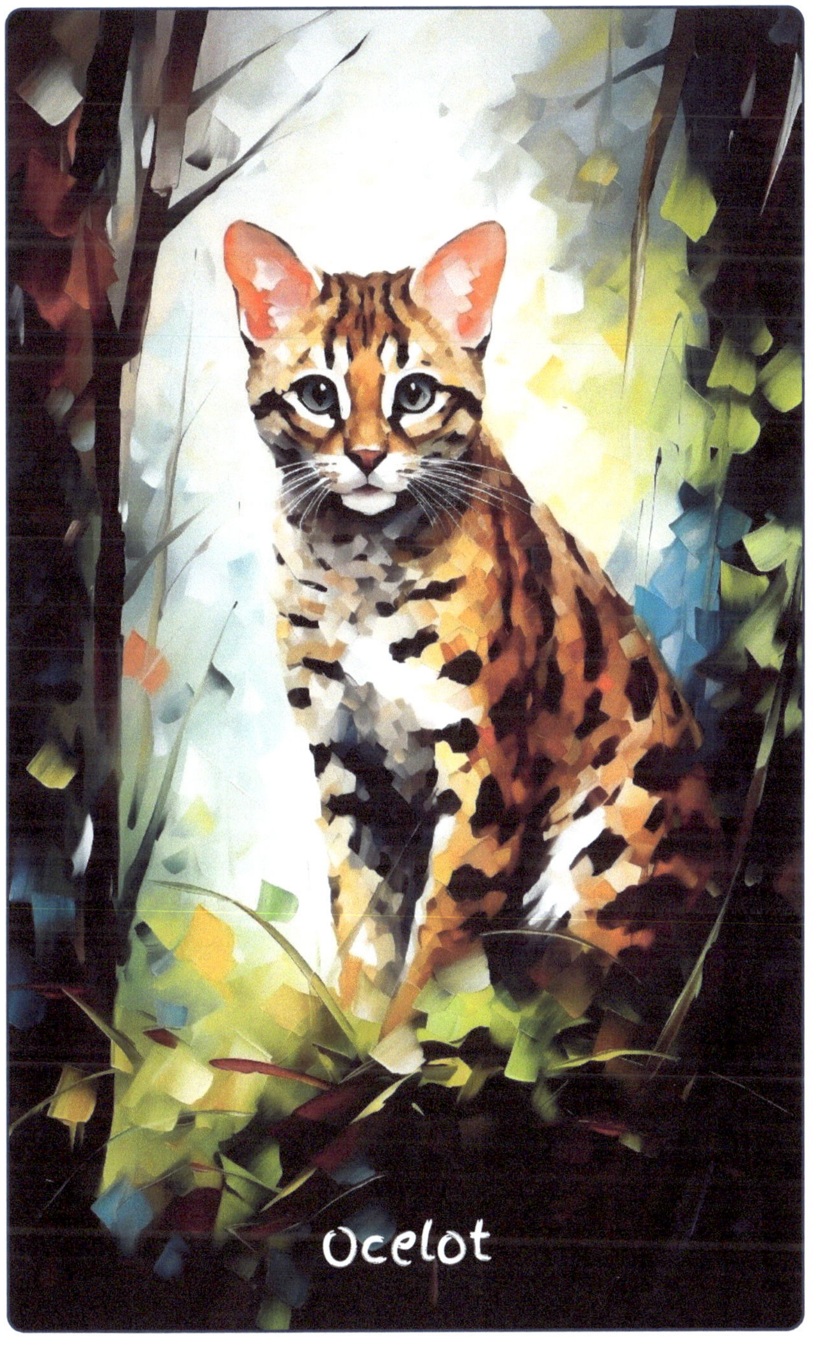

Ocelot

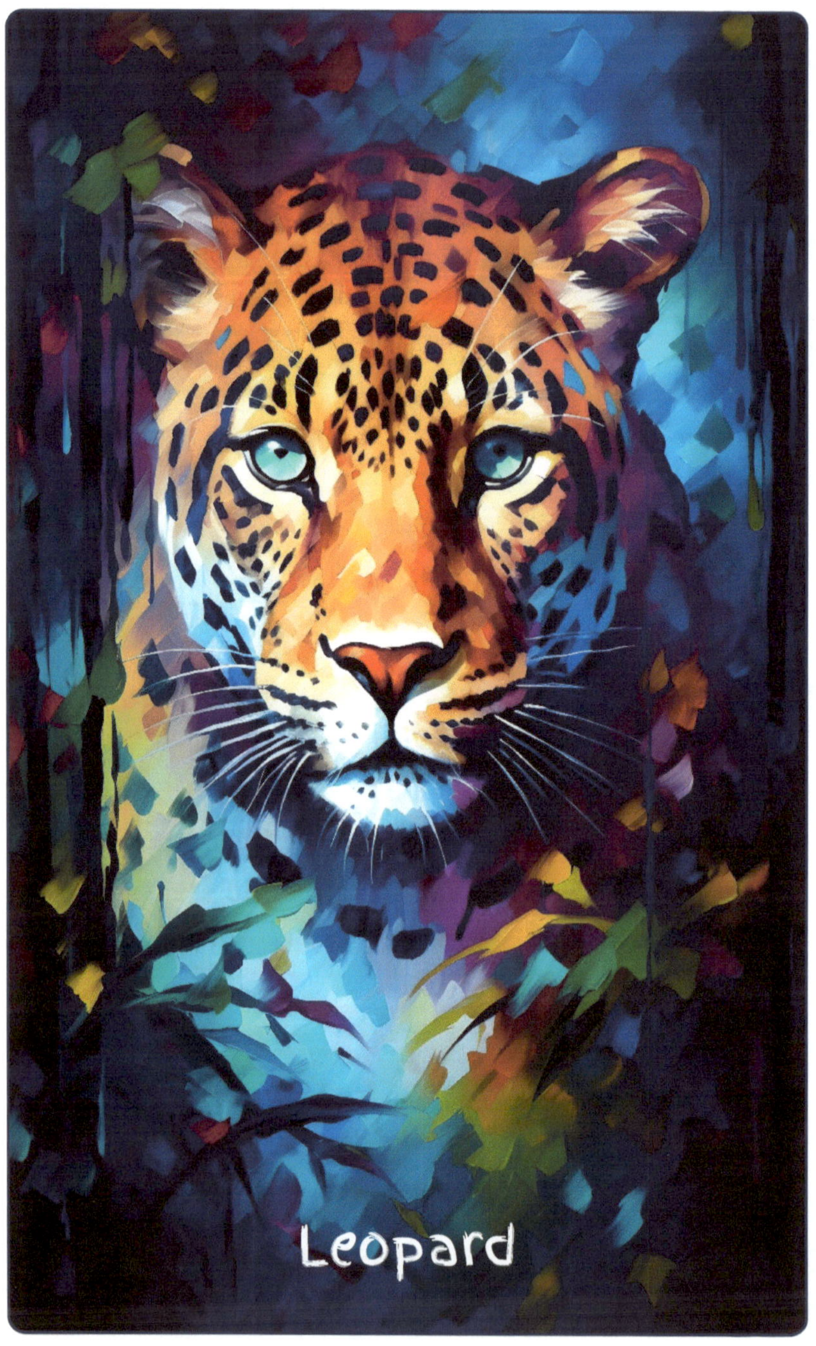

Leopard

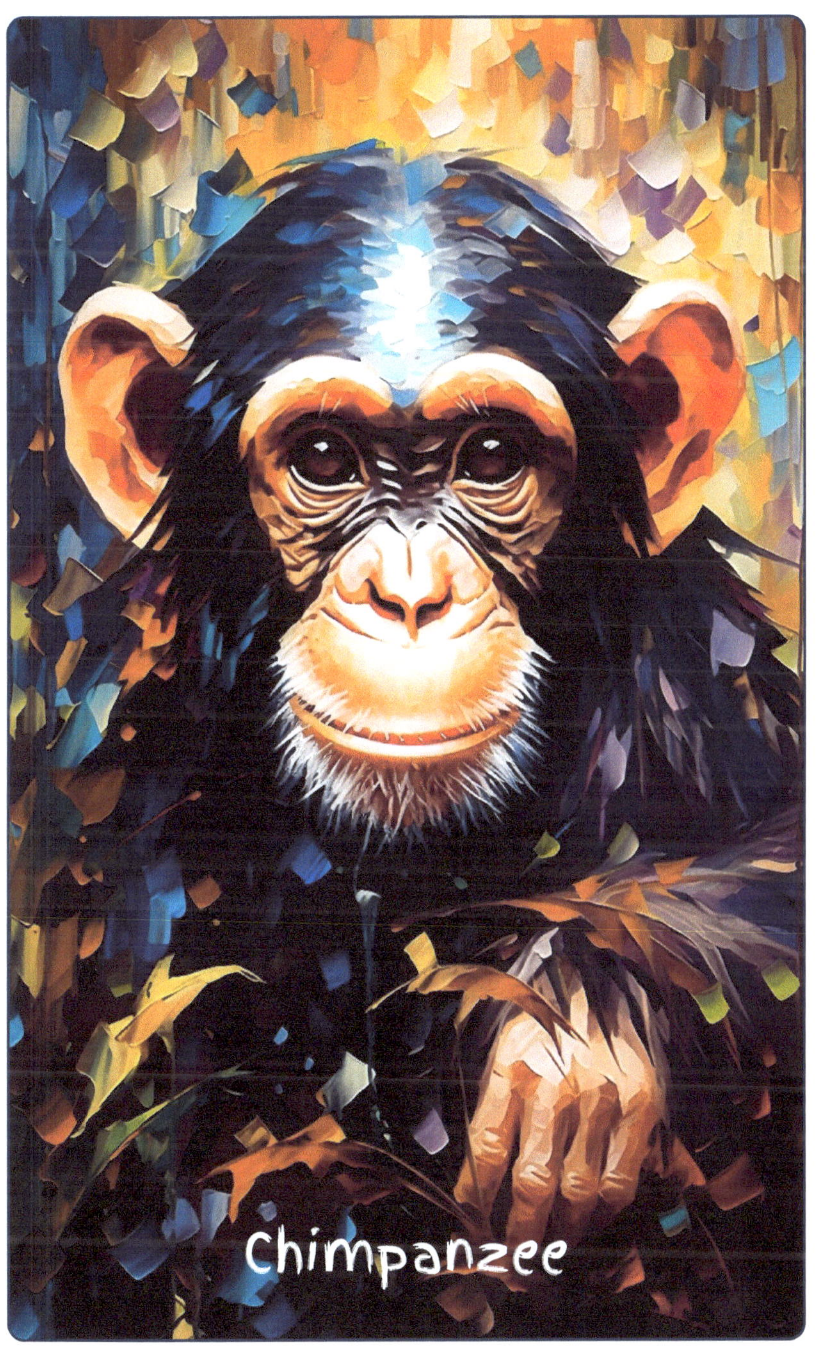

Chimpanzee

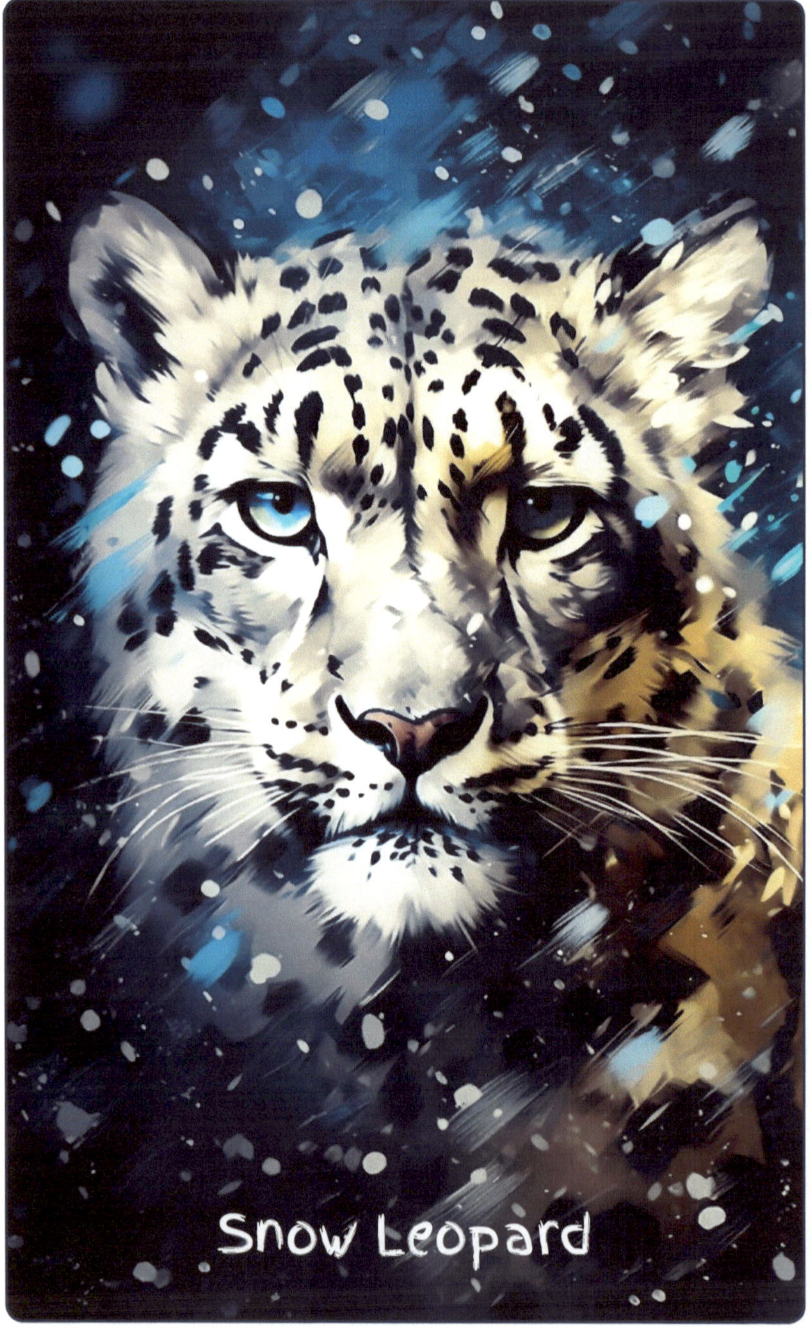

Snow Leopard

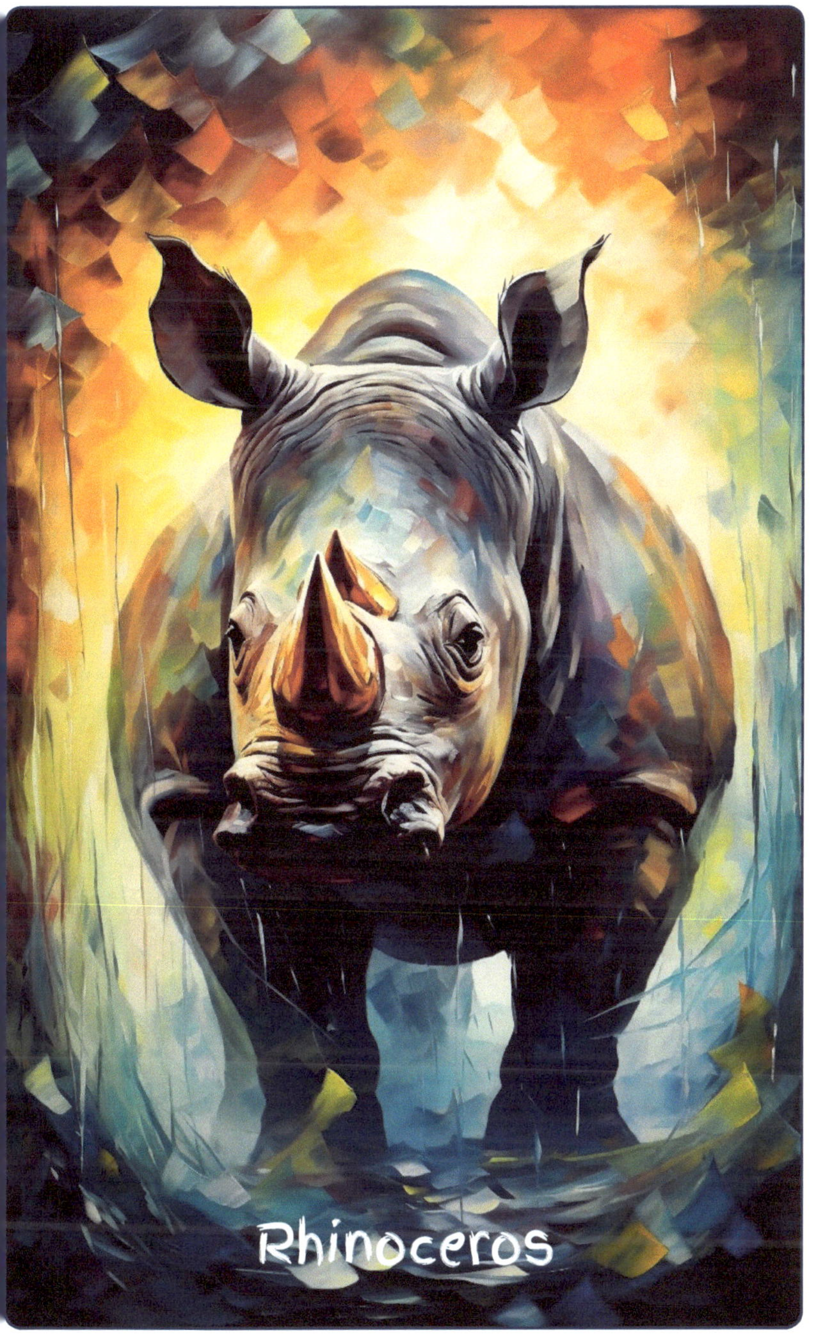
Rhinoceros

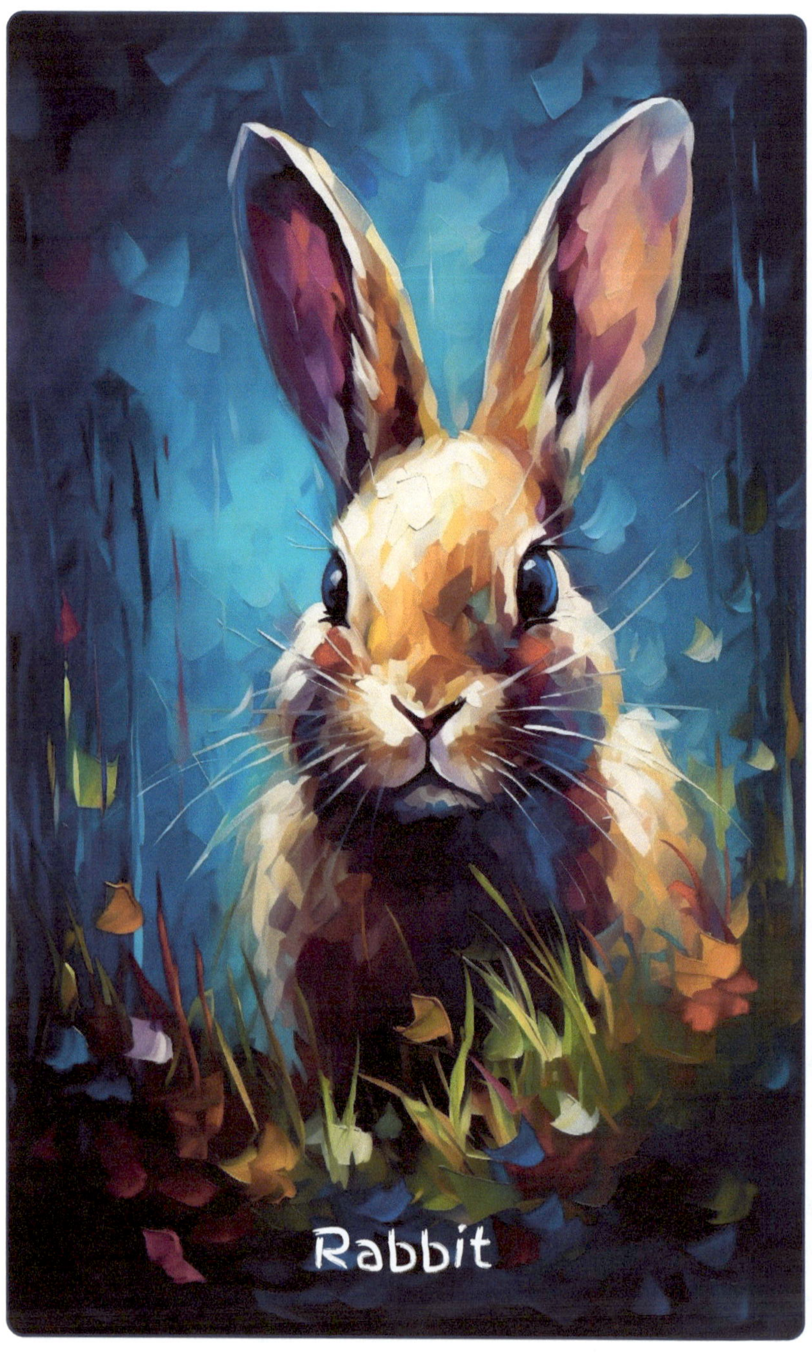

Rabbit

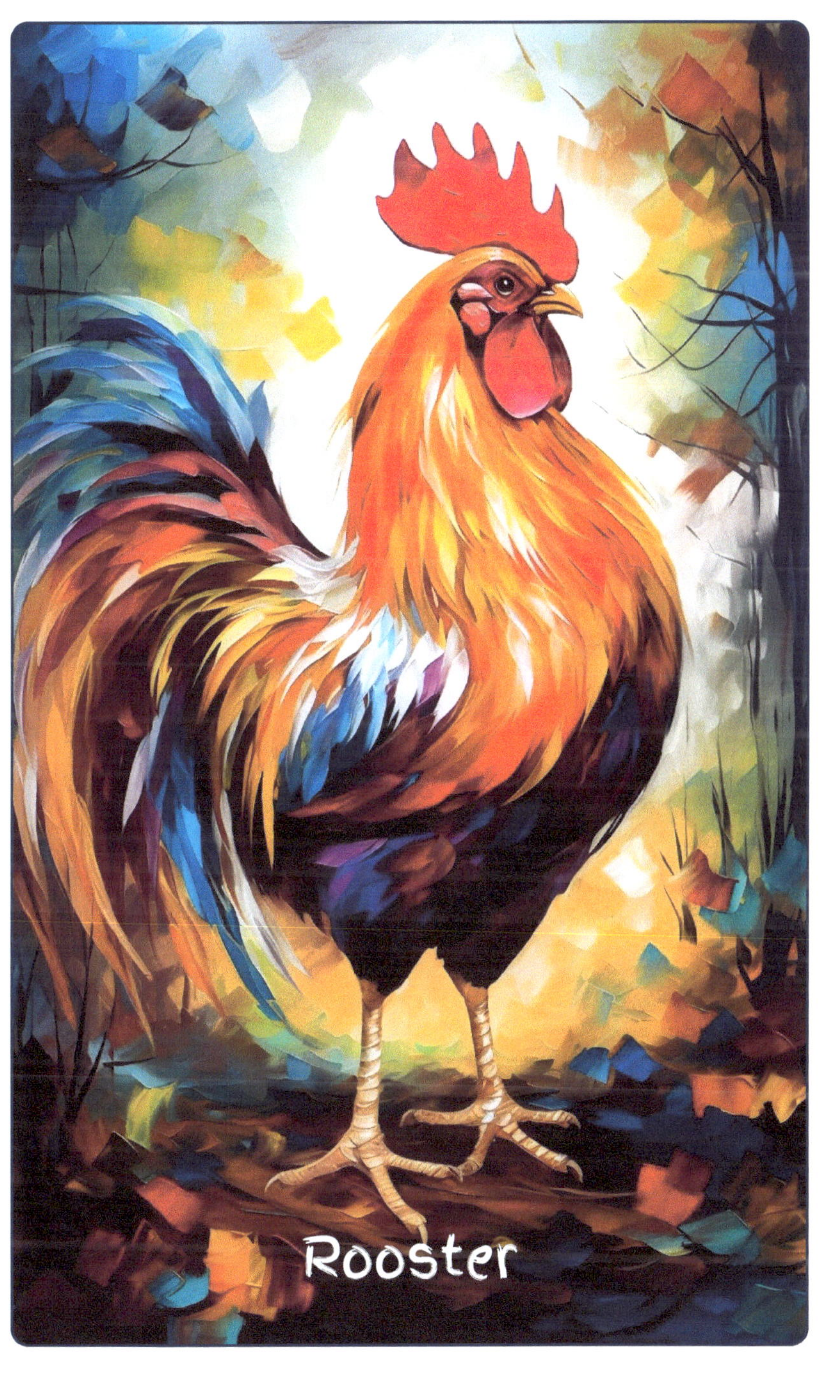

Rooster

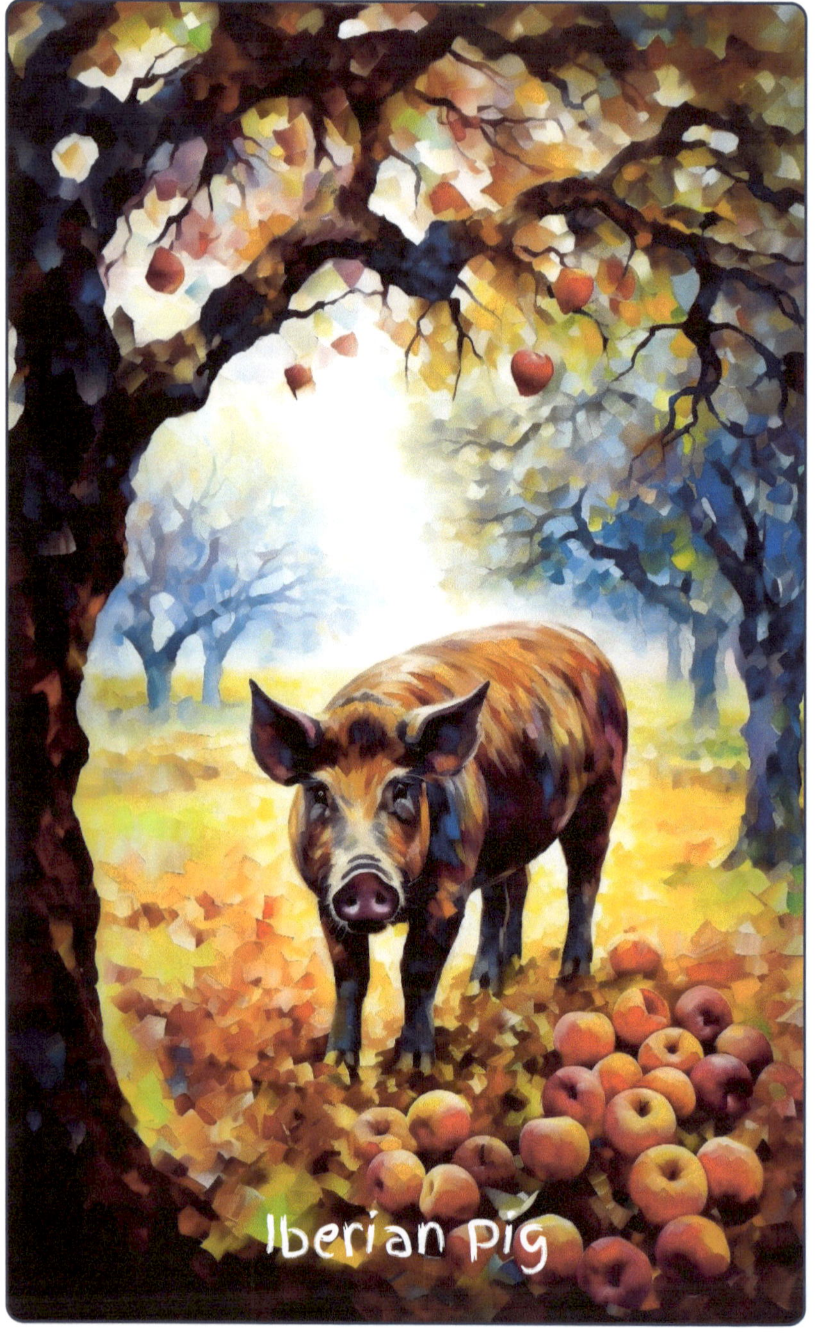

Iberian pig

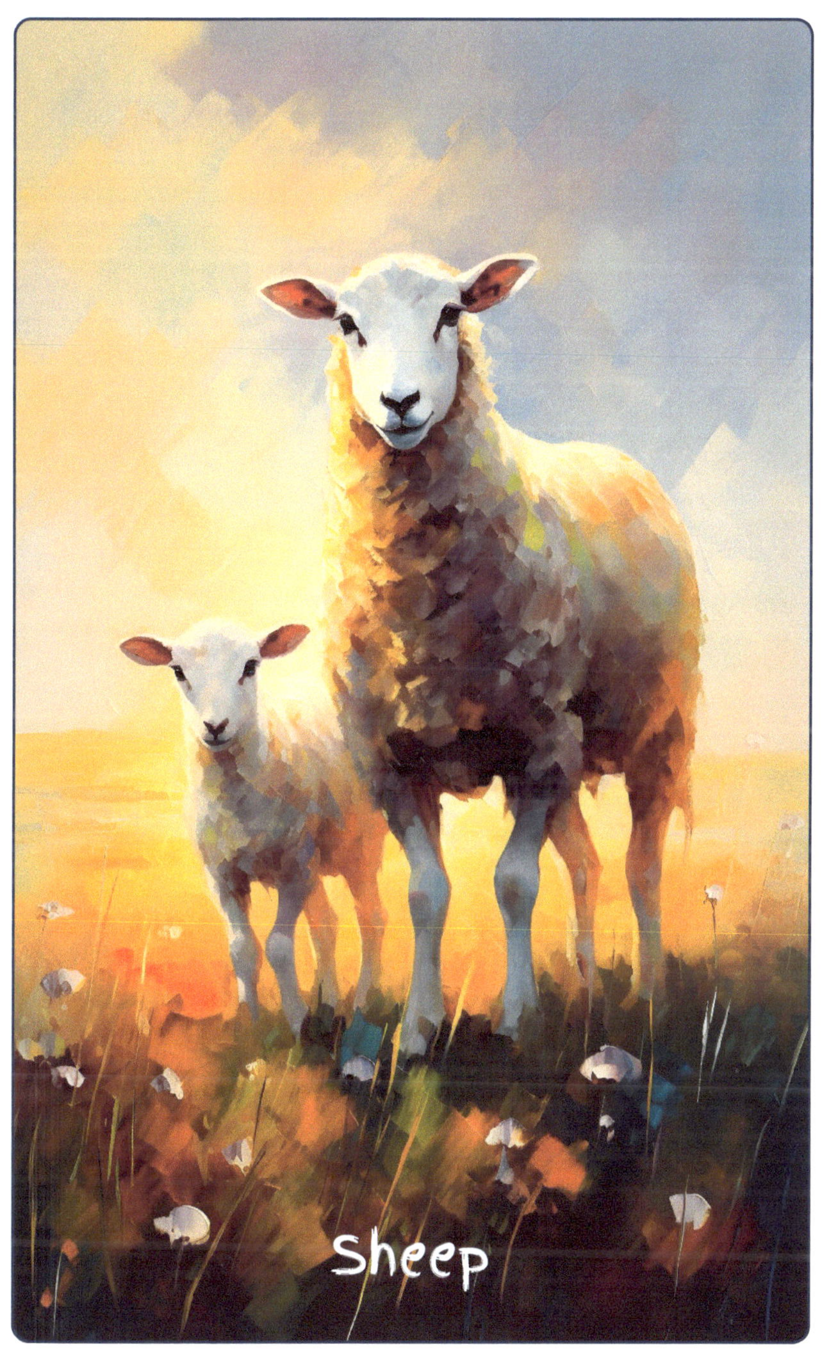

Sheep

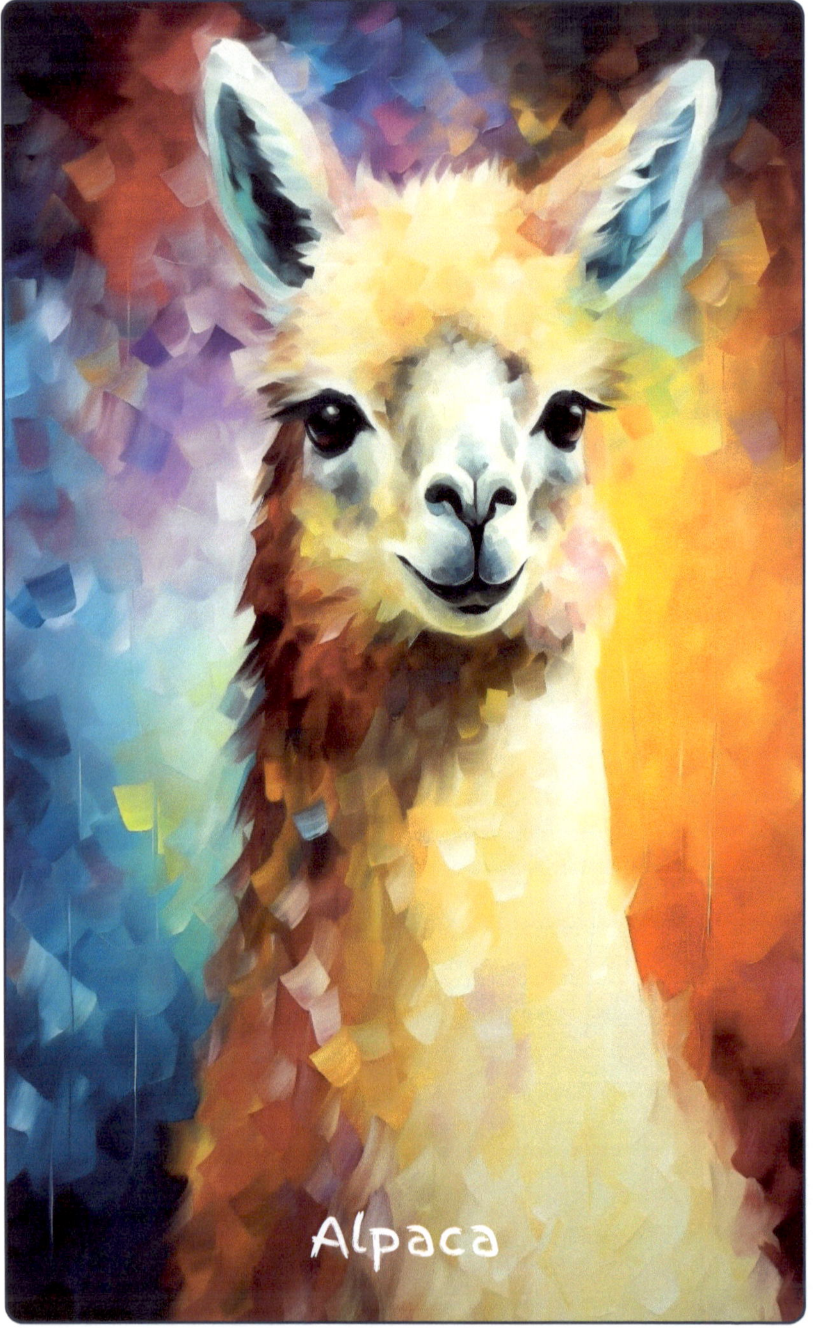
Alpaca

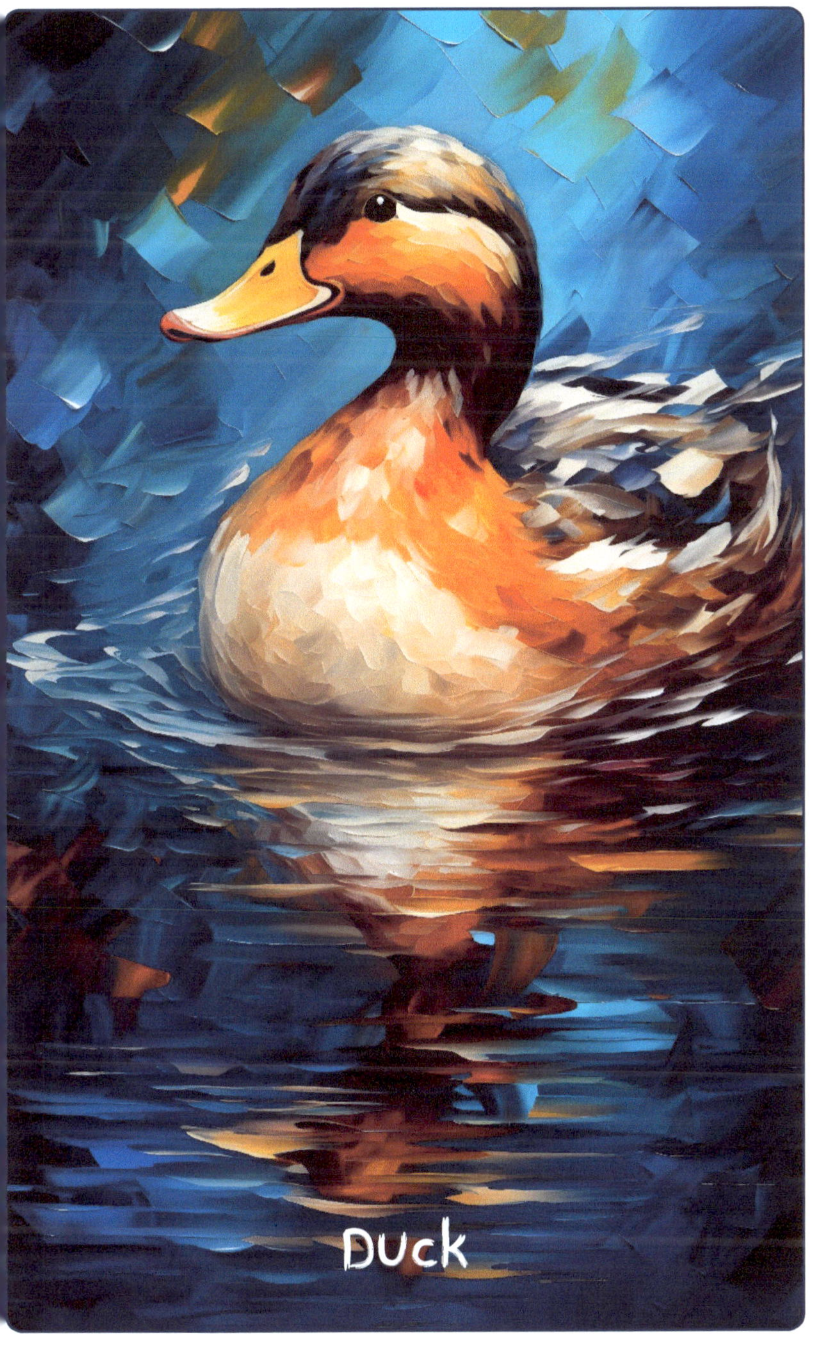

Duck

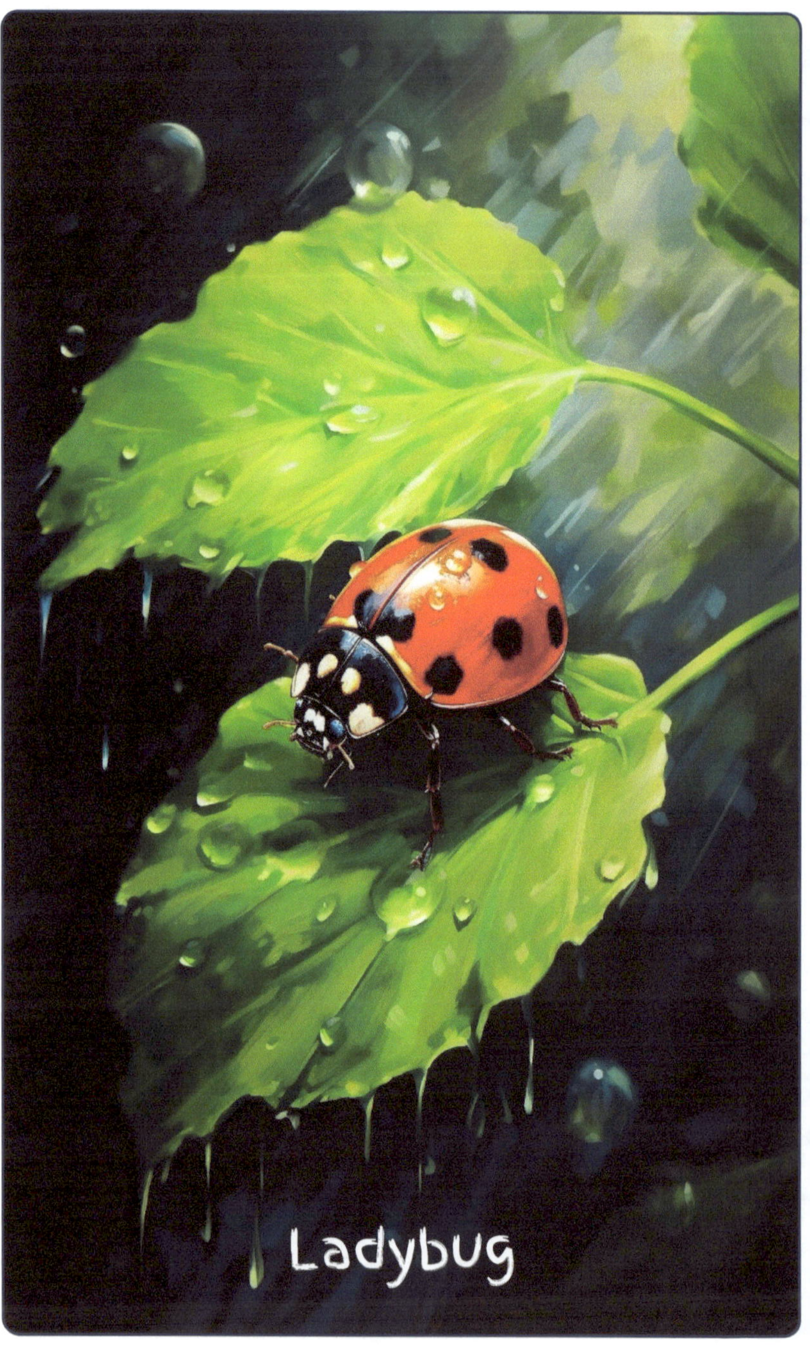

Ladybug

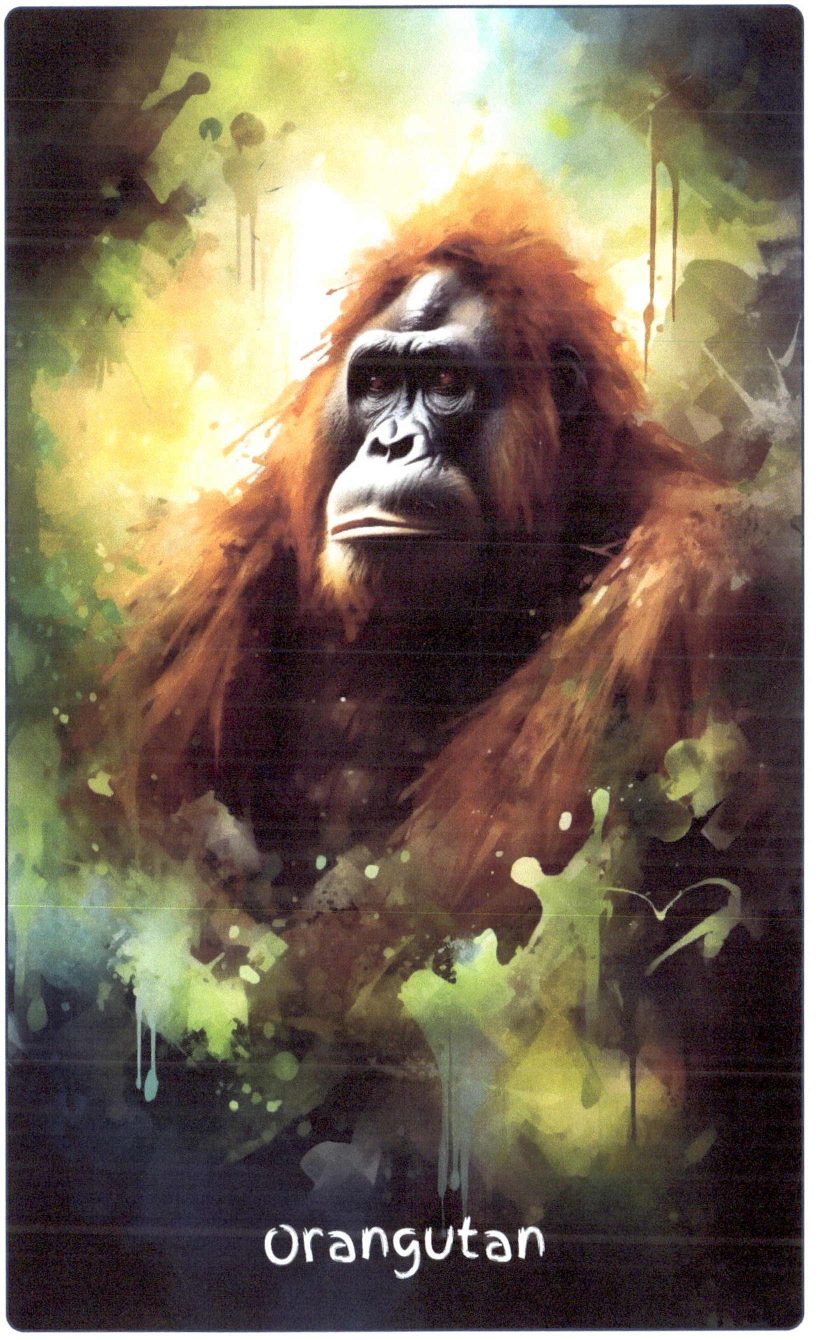

Orangutan

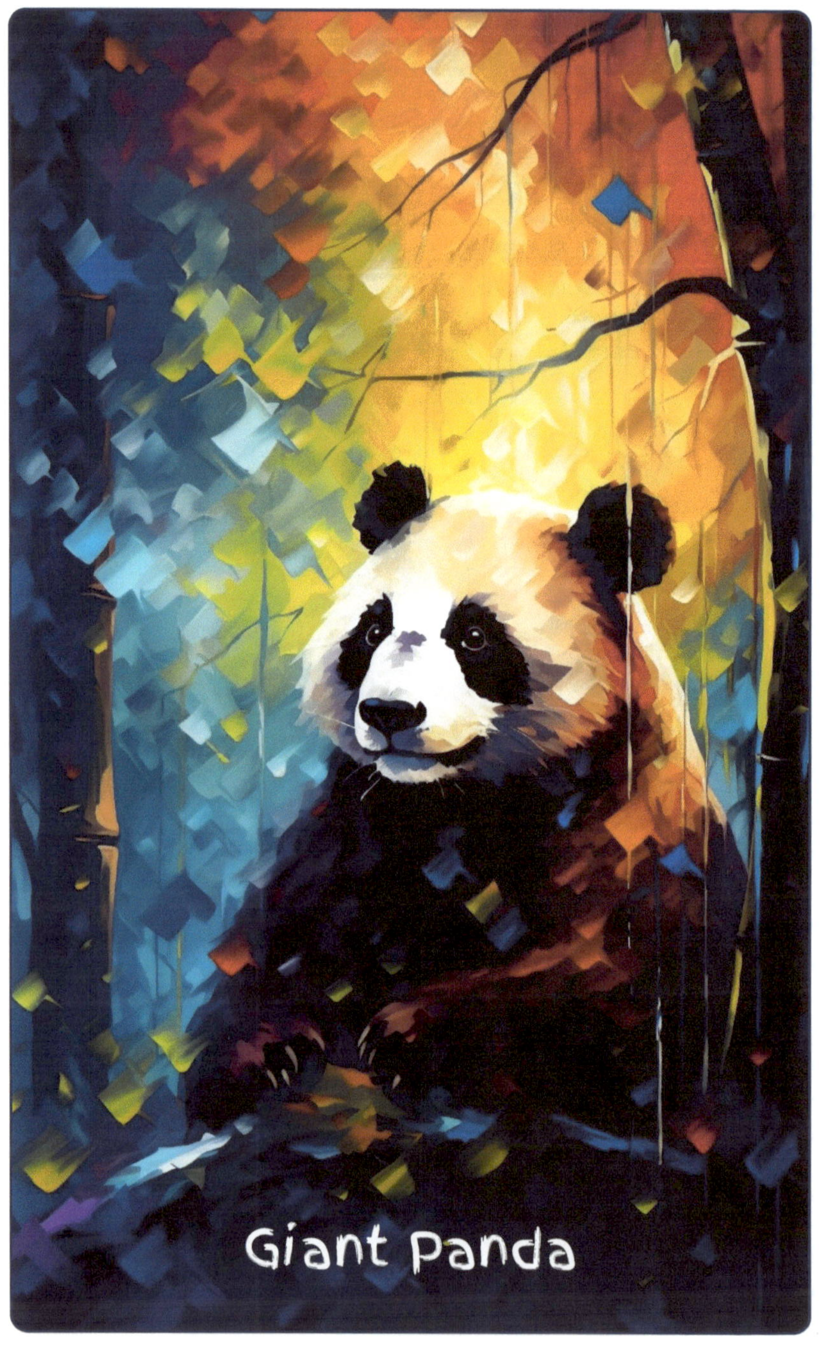

Giant panda

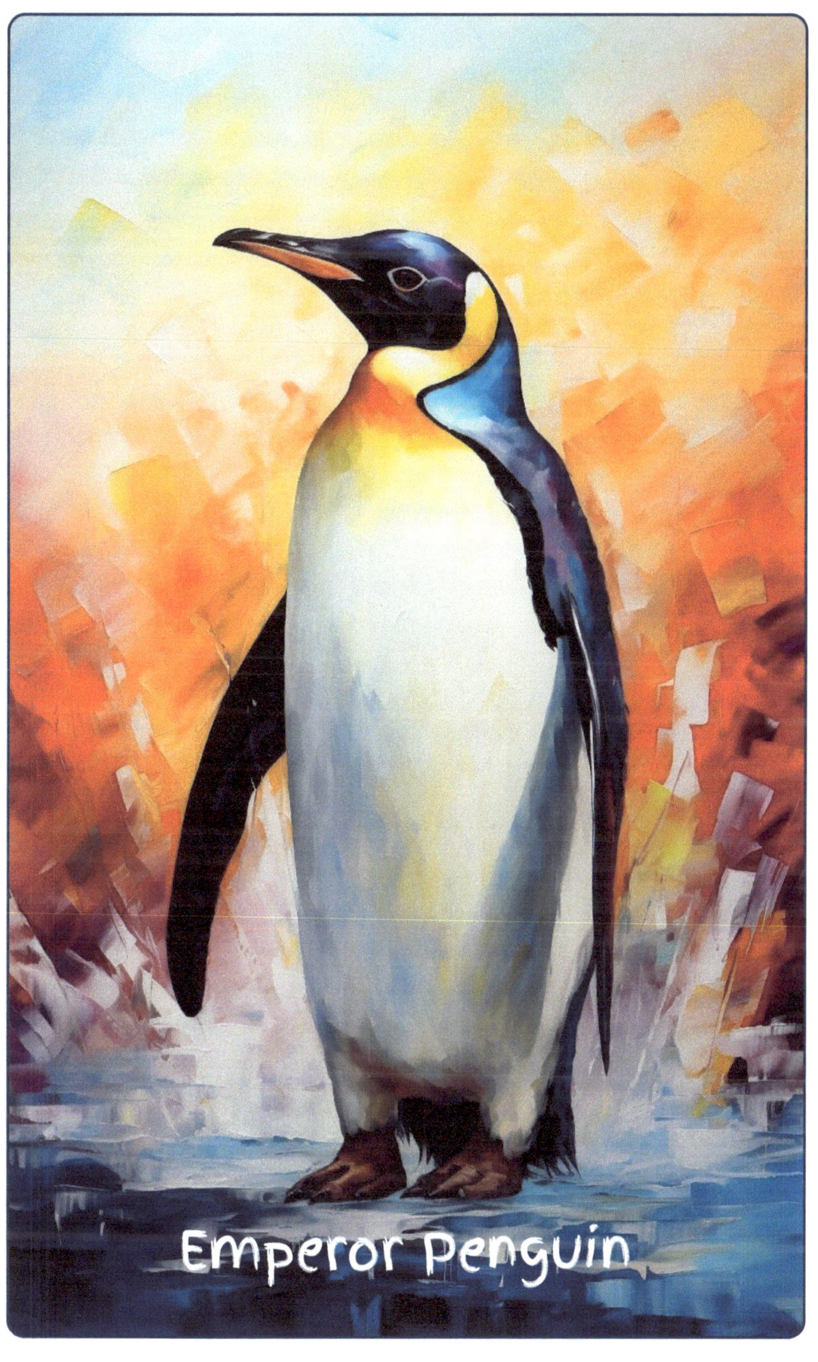

Emperor Penguin

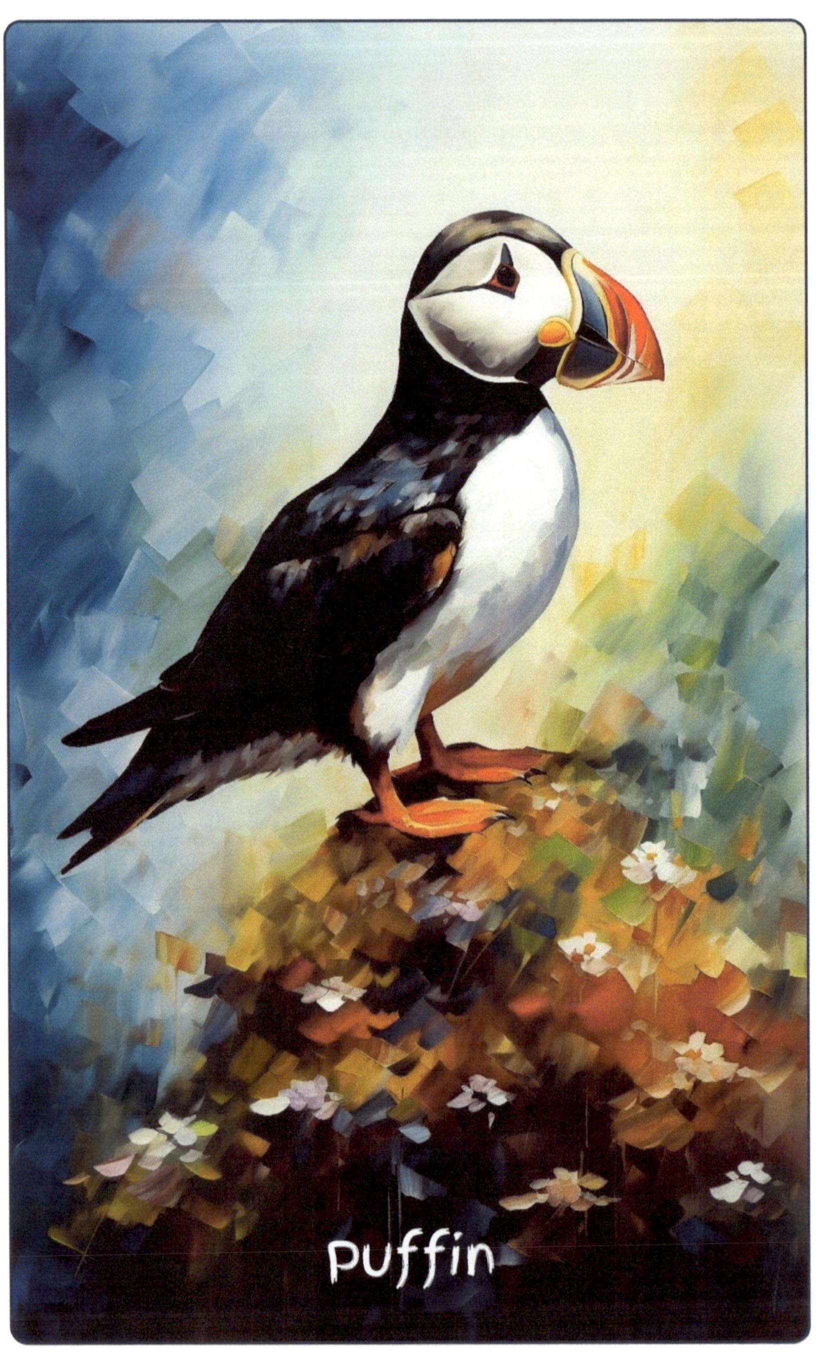
puffin

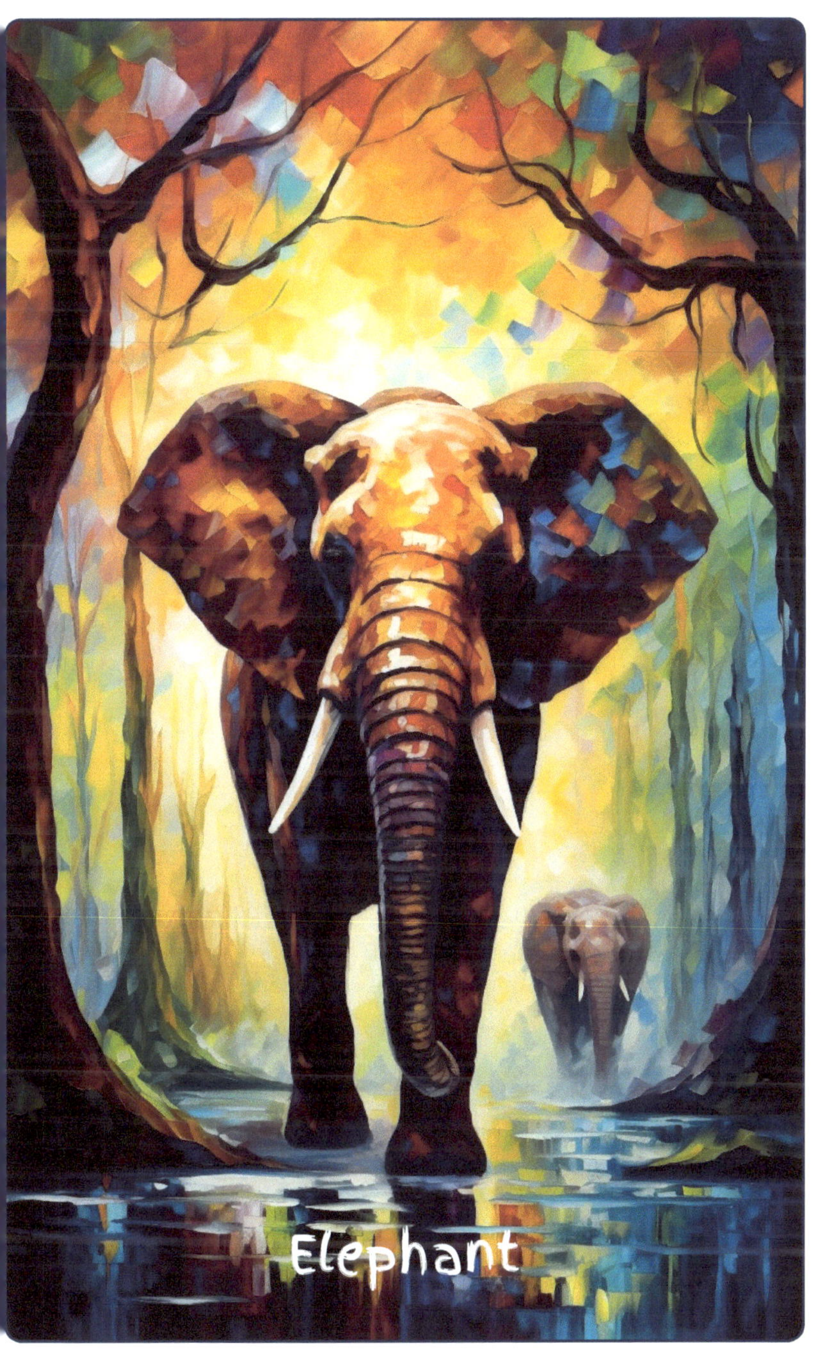

Elephant

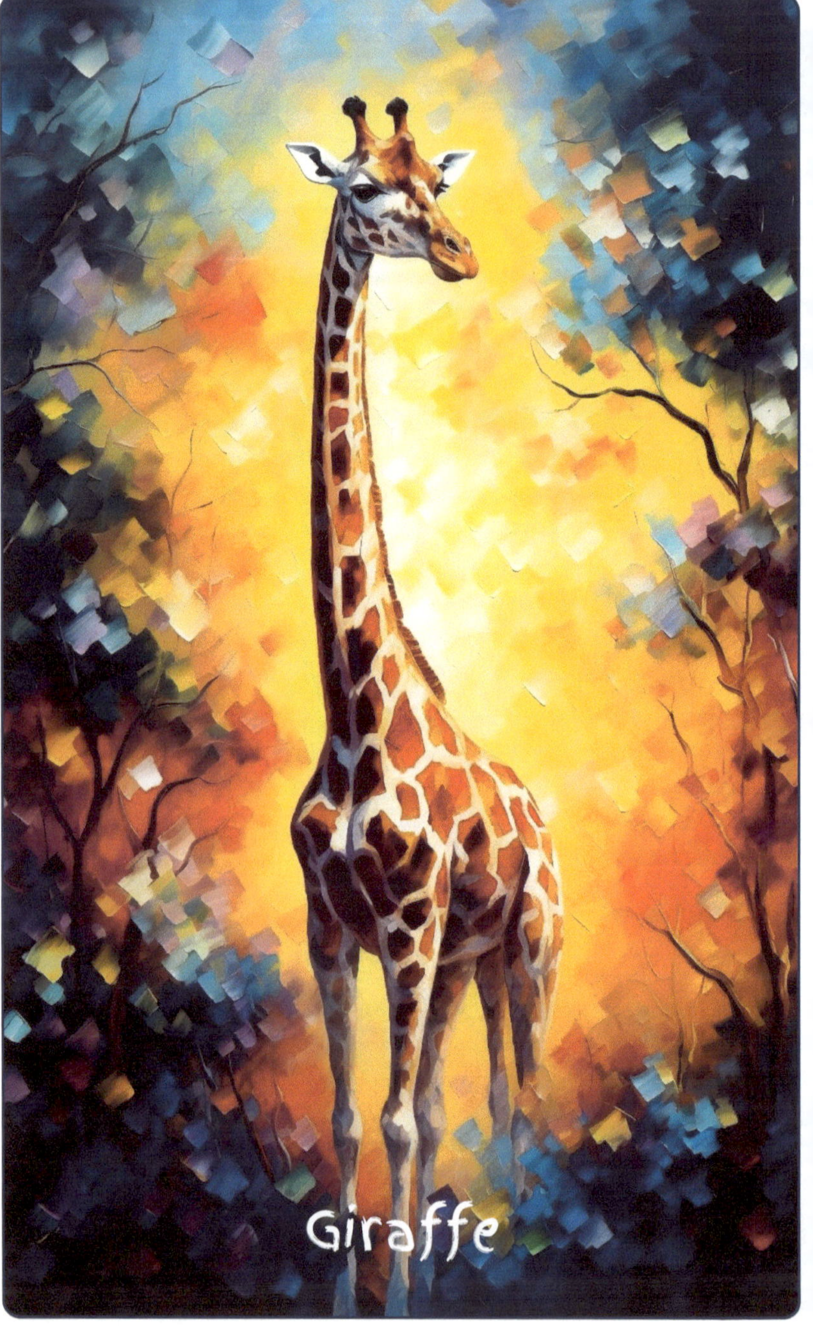
Giraffe

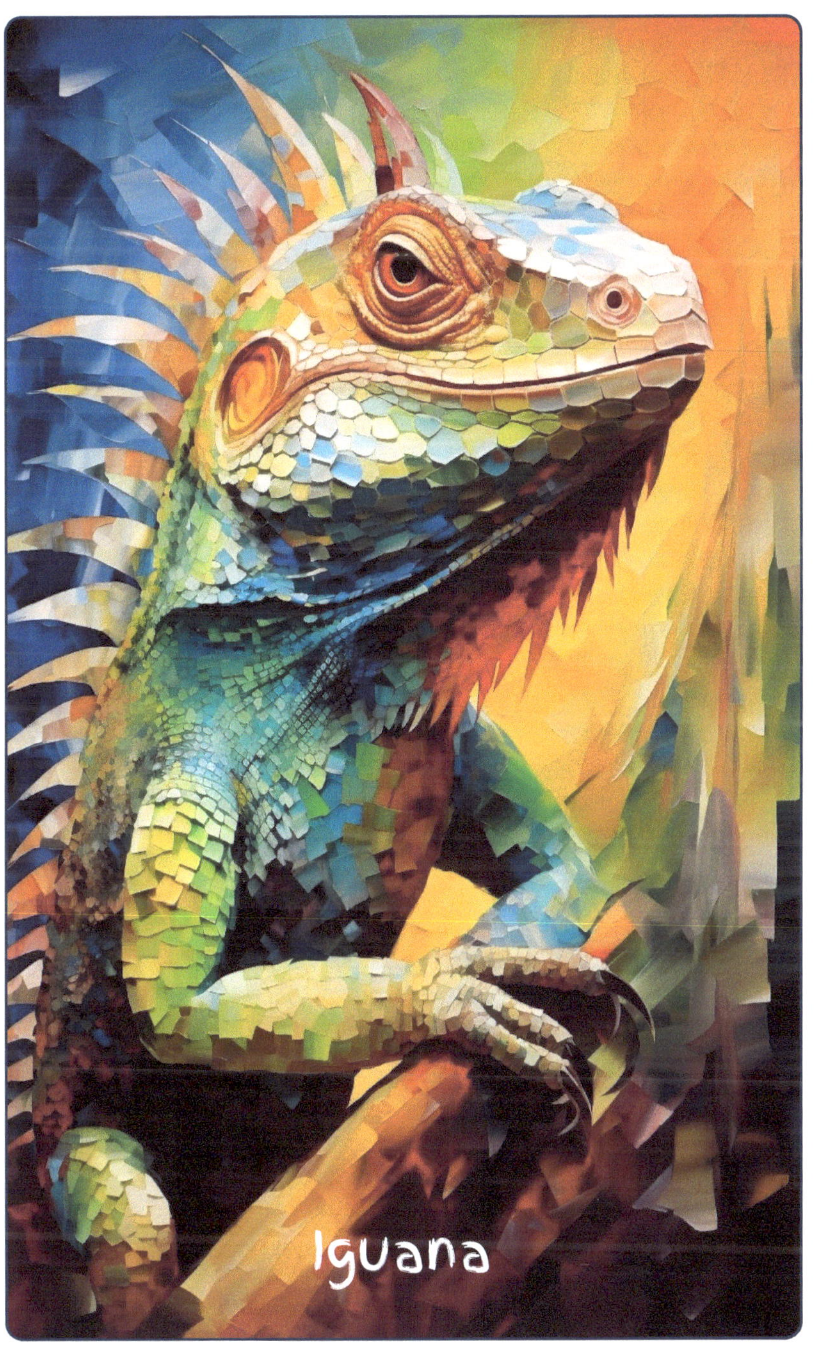

Iguana

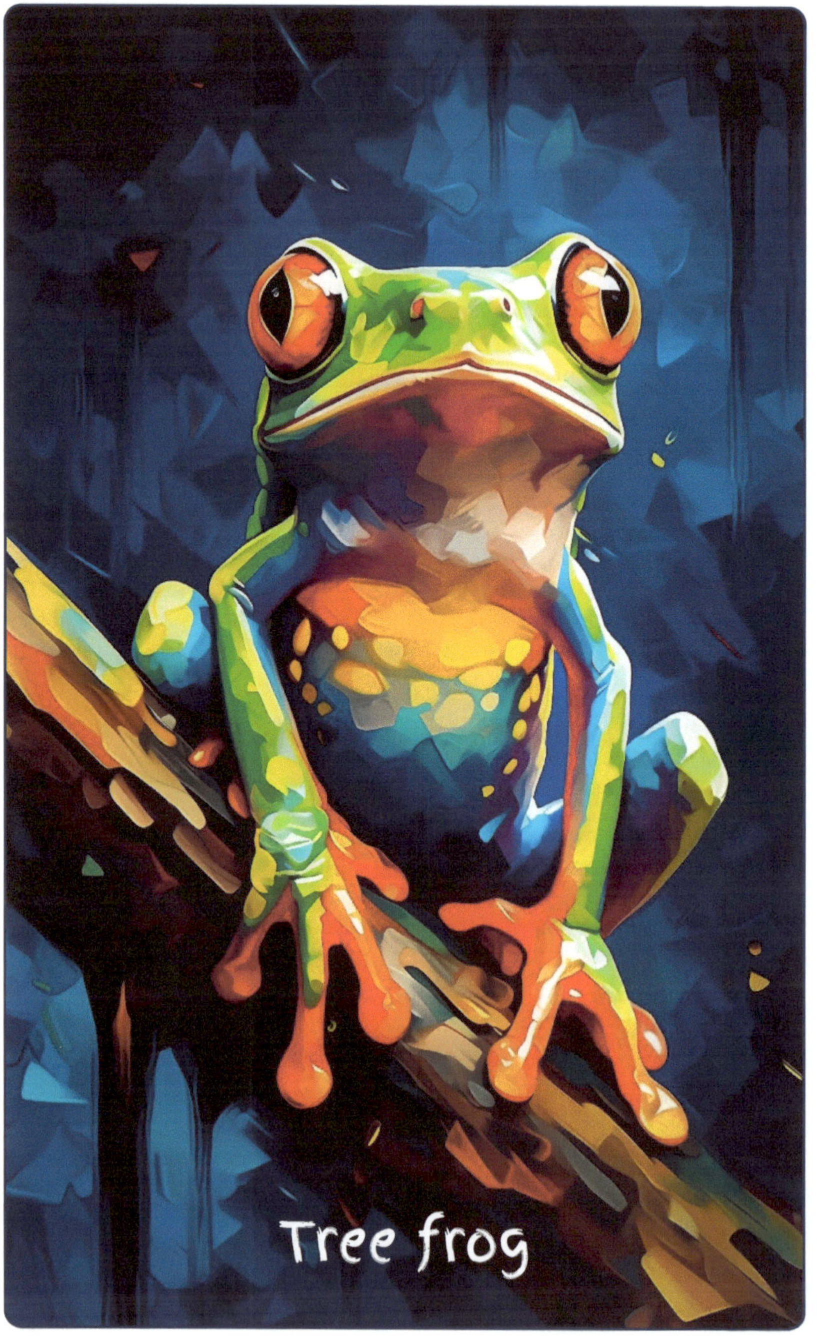

Tree frog

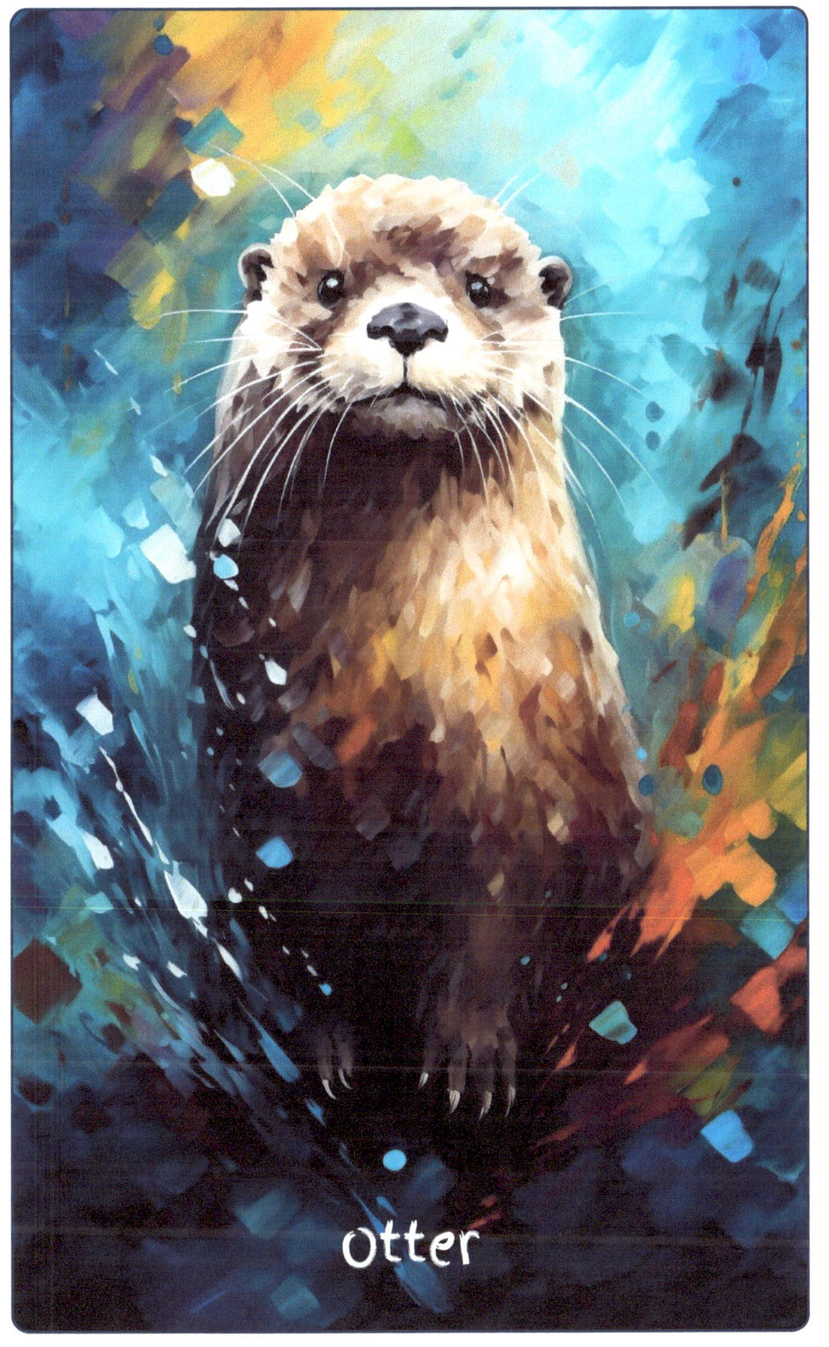

Otter

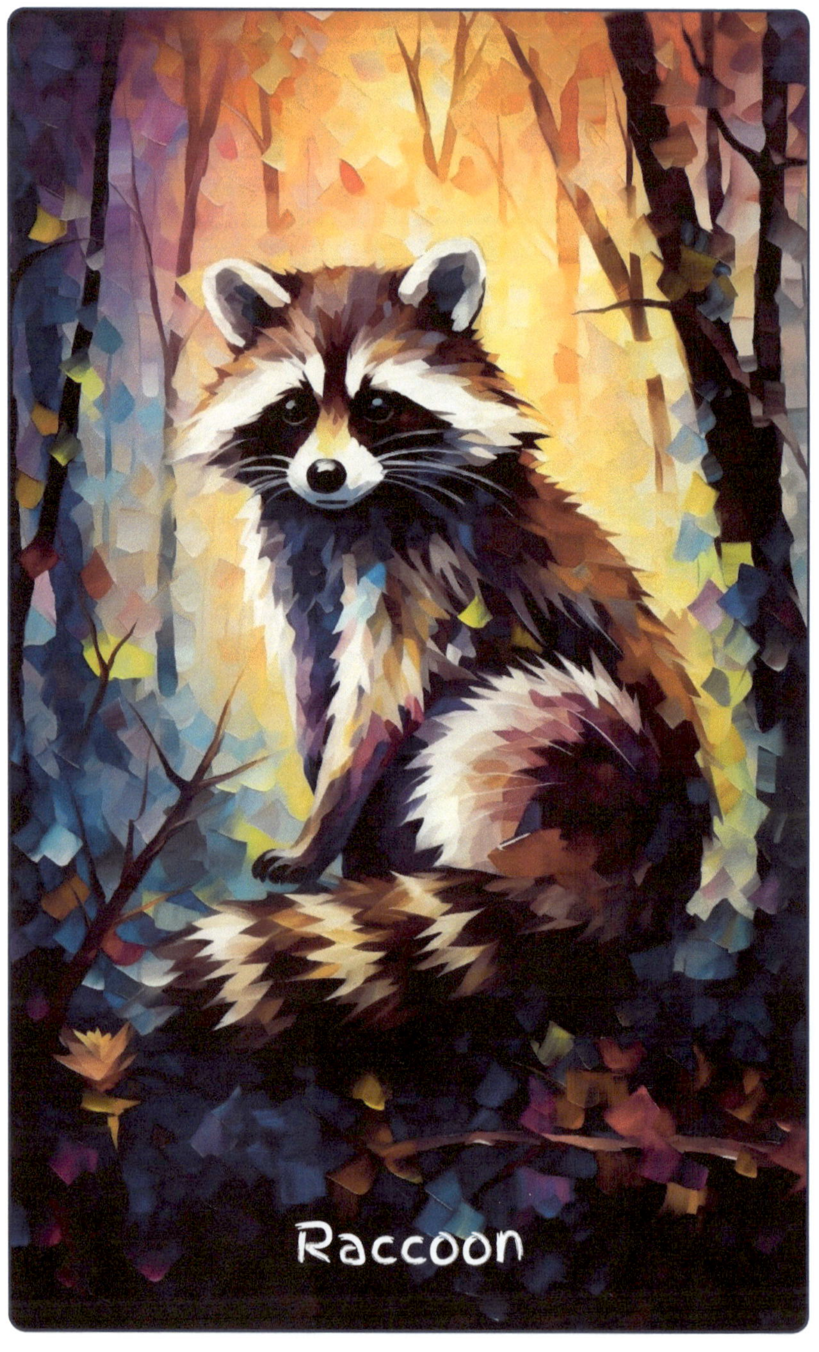

Raccoon

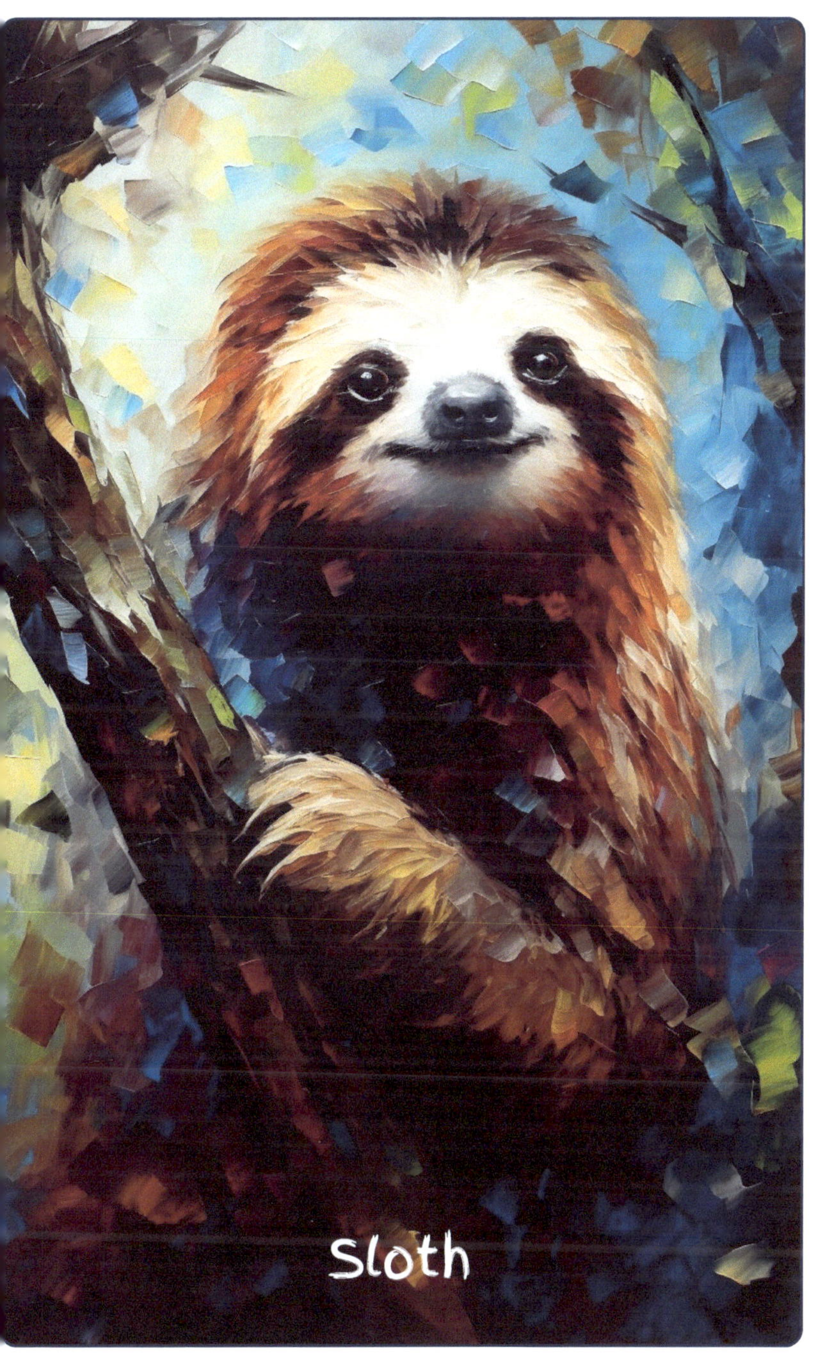

Sloth

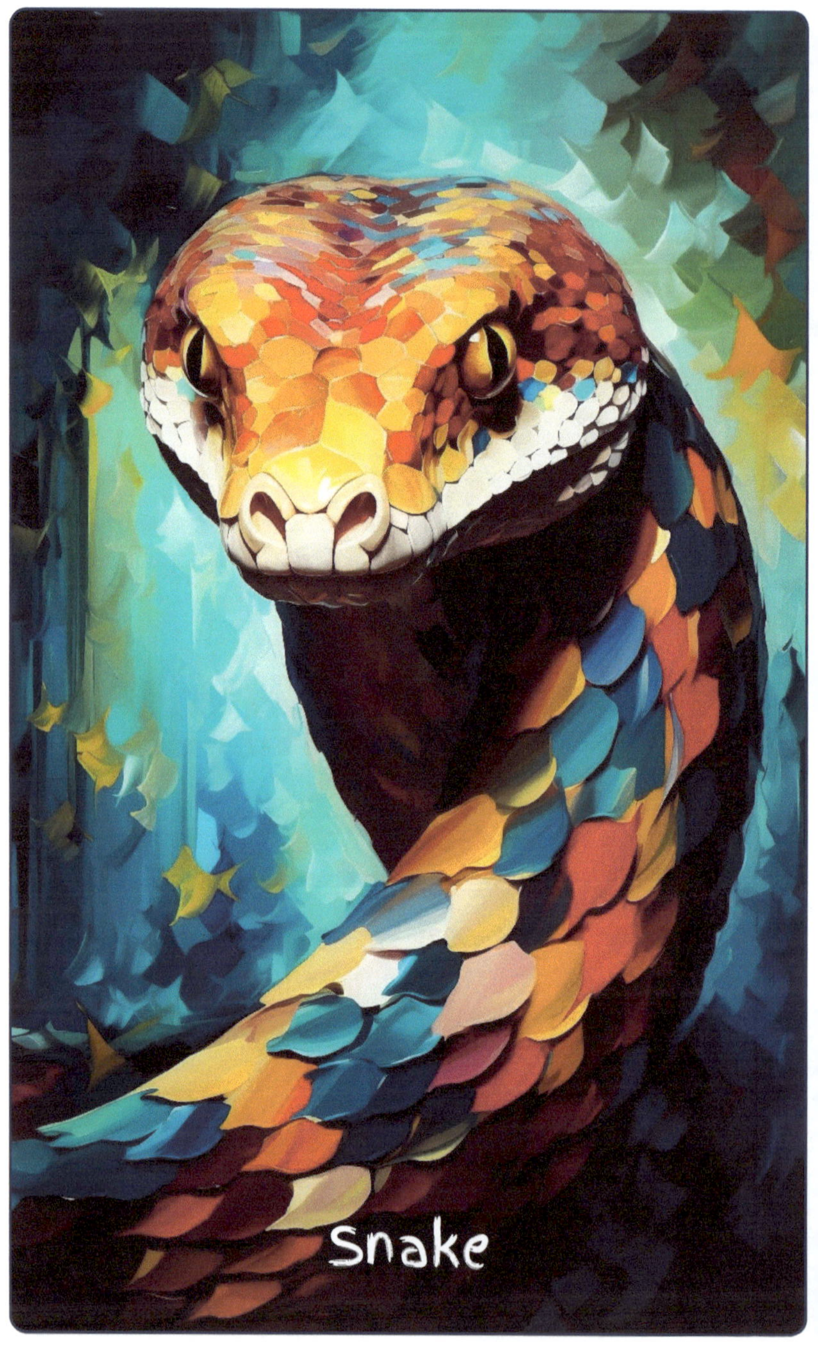

Snake

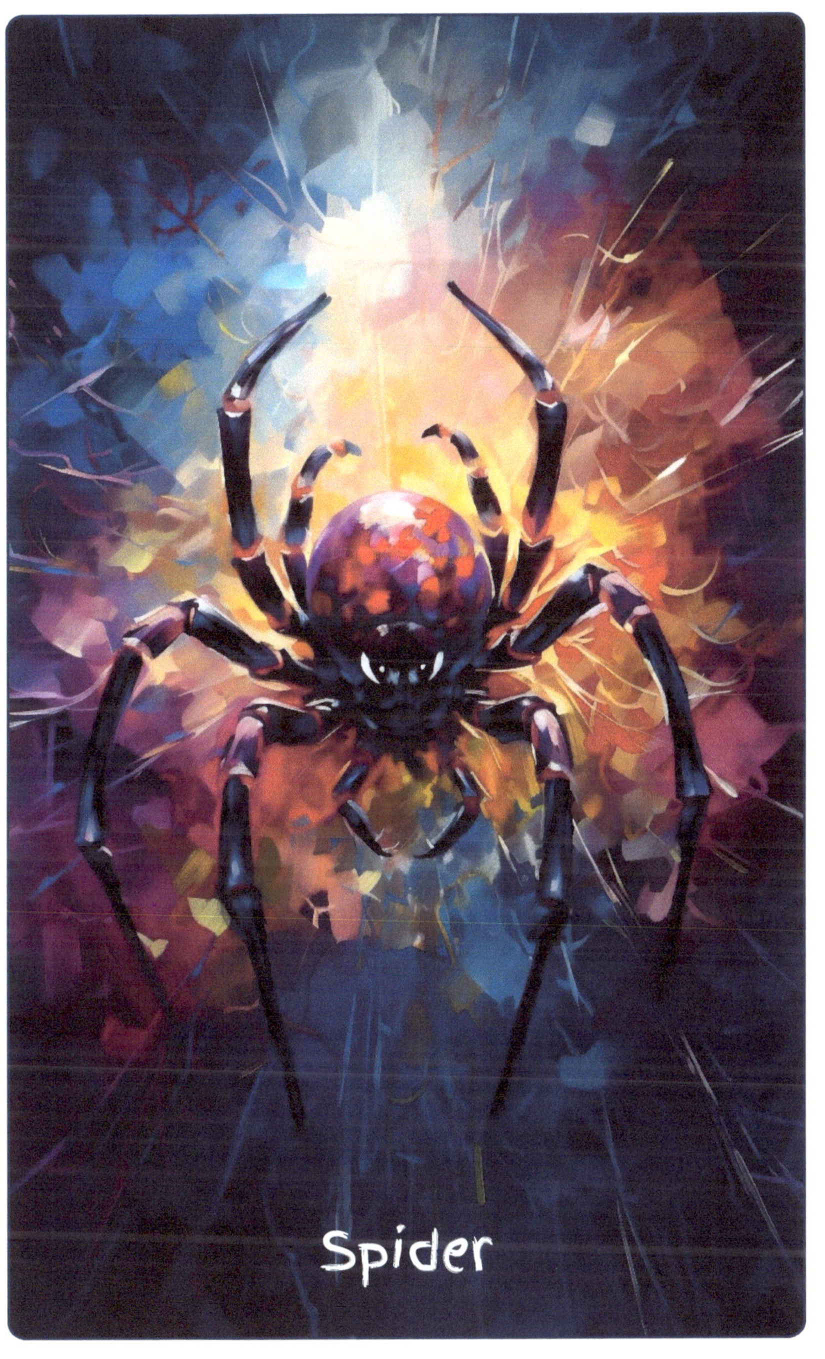

Spider

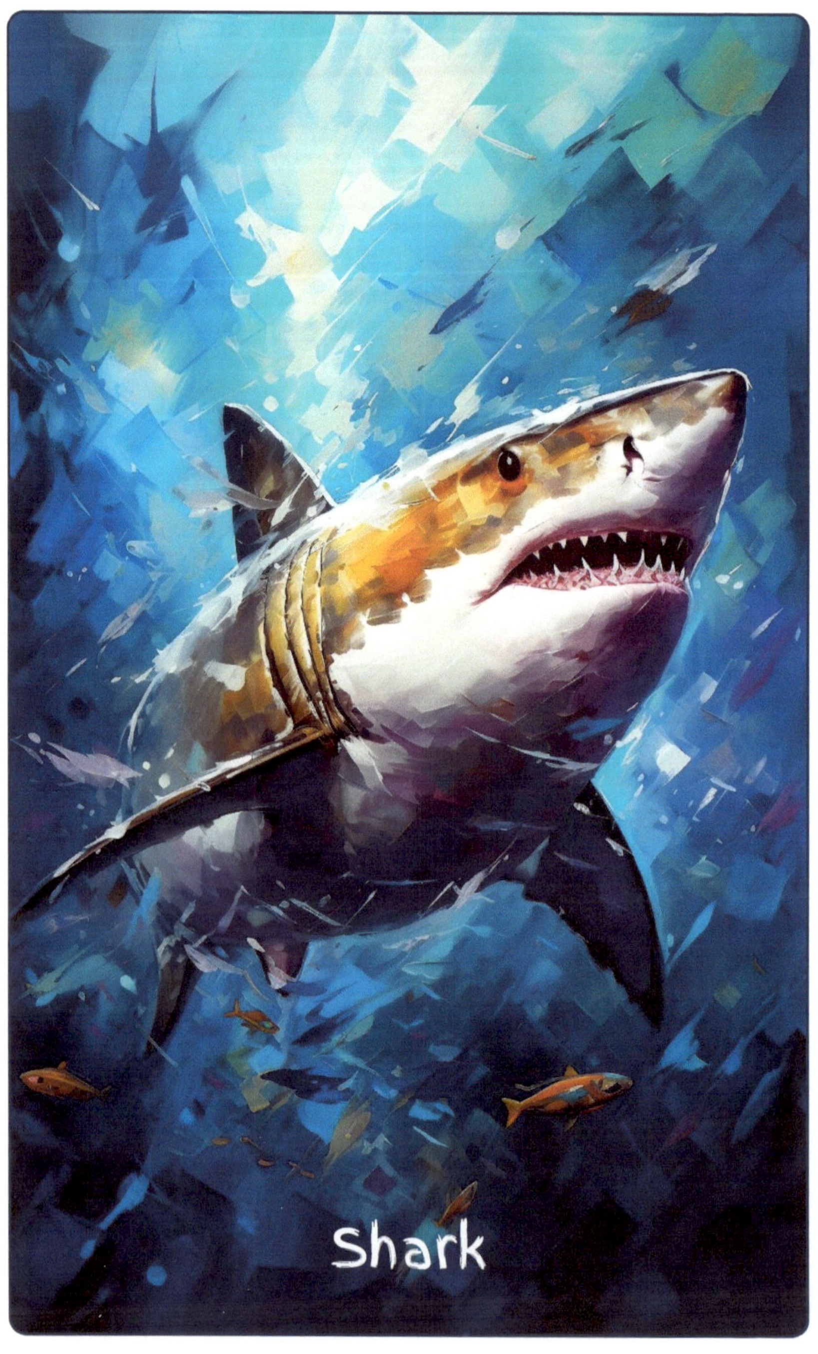

Shark

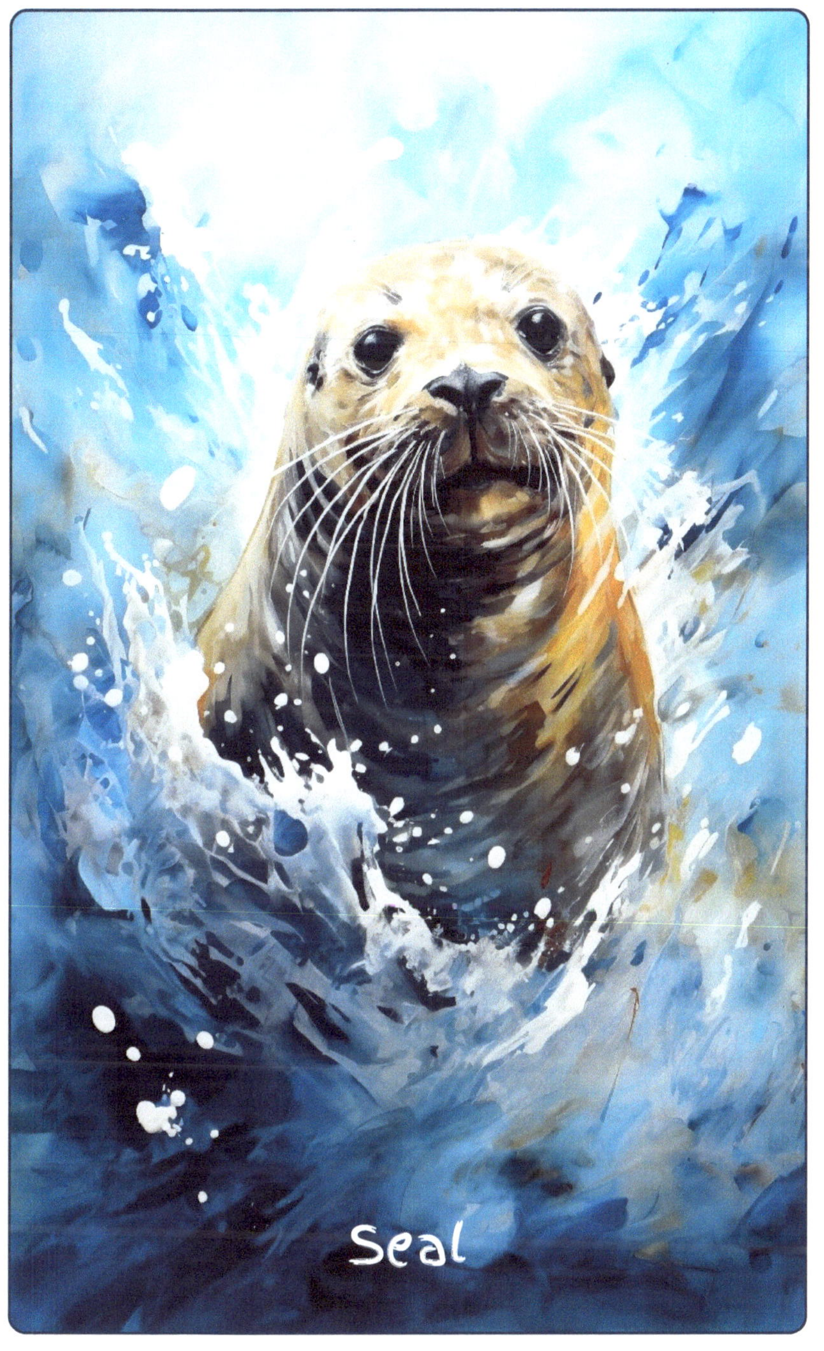

Seal

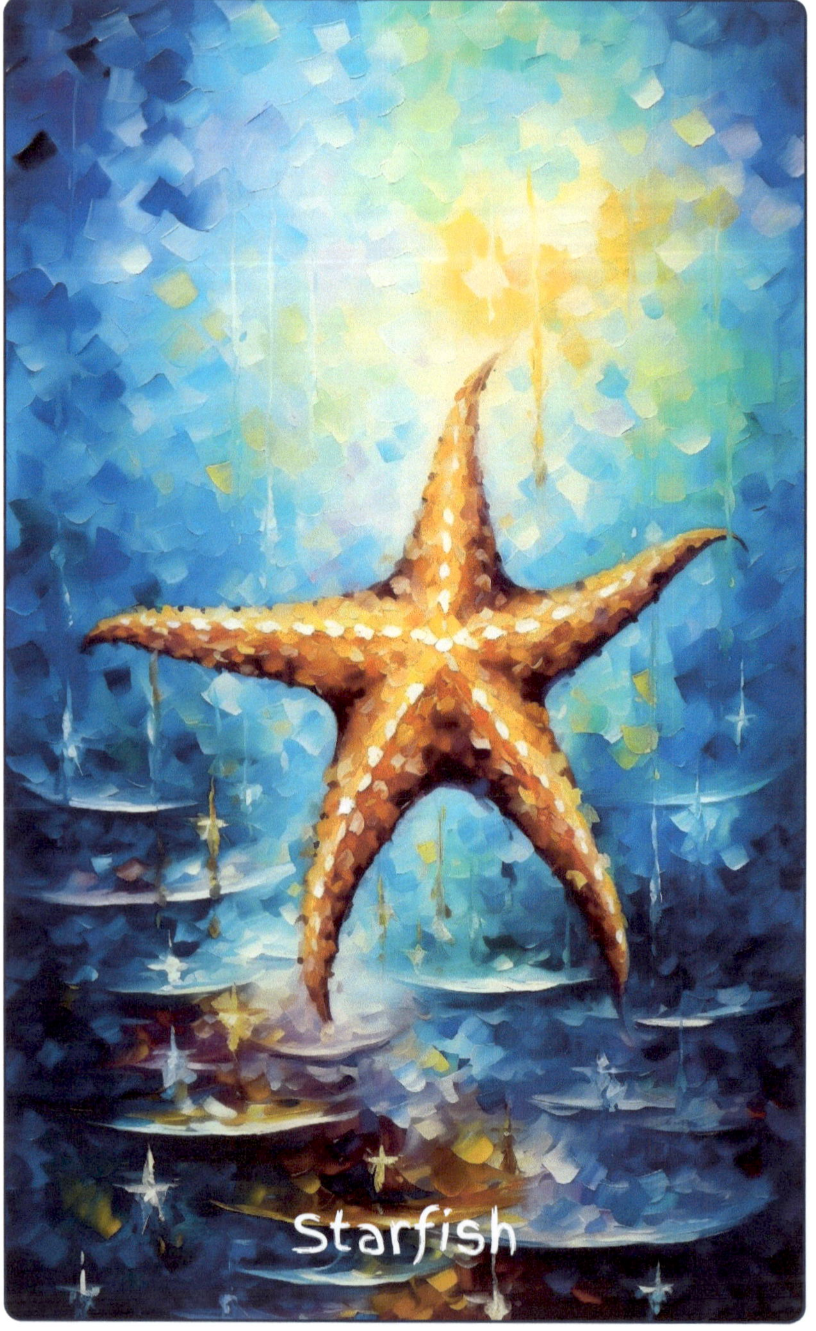
Starfish

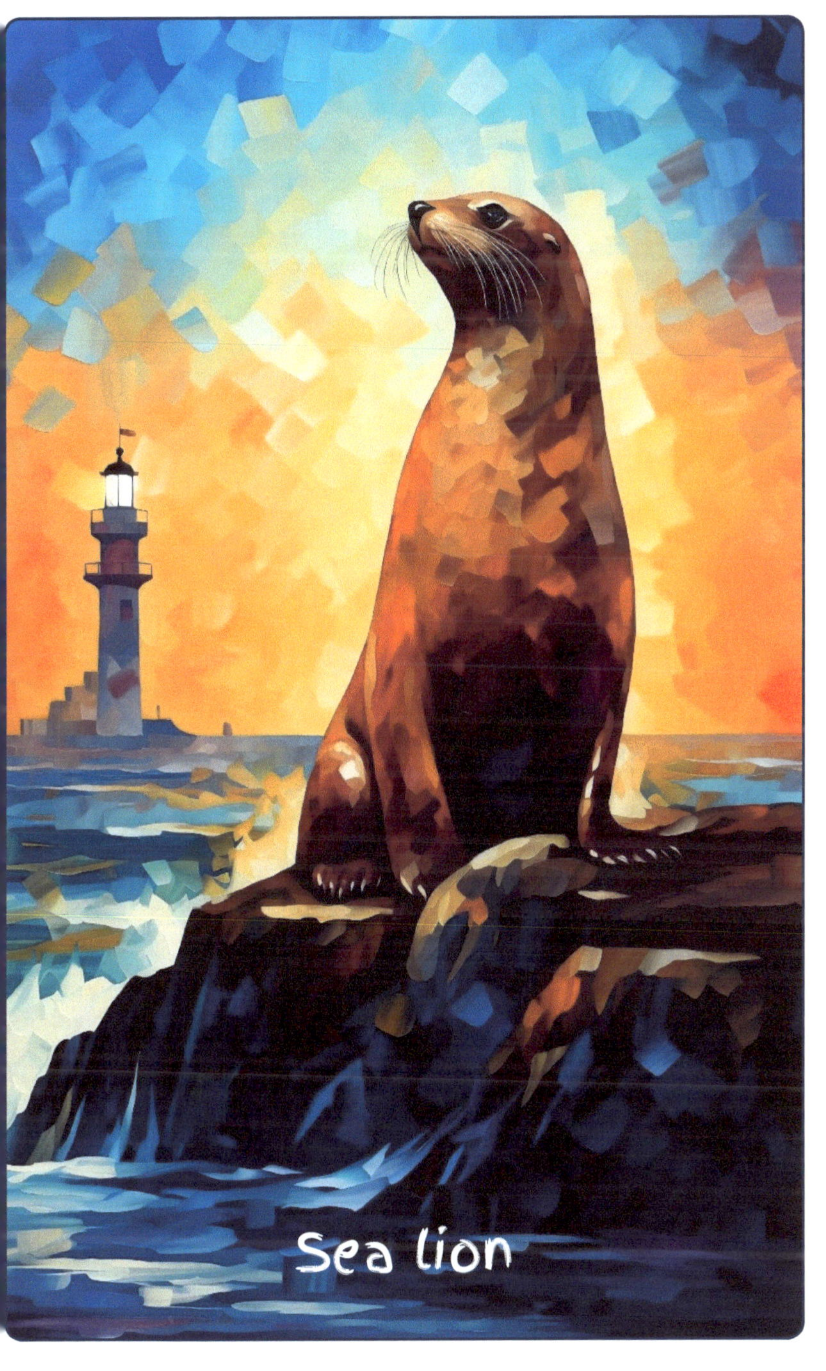

Sea lion

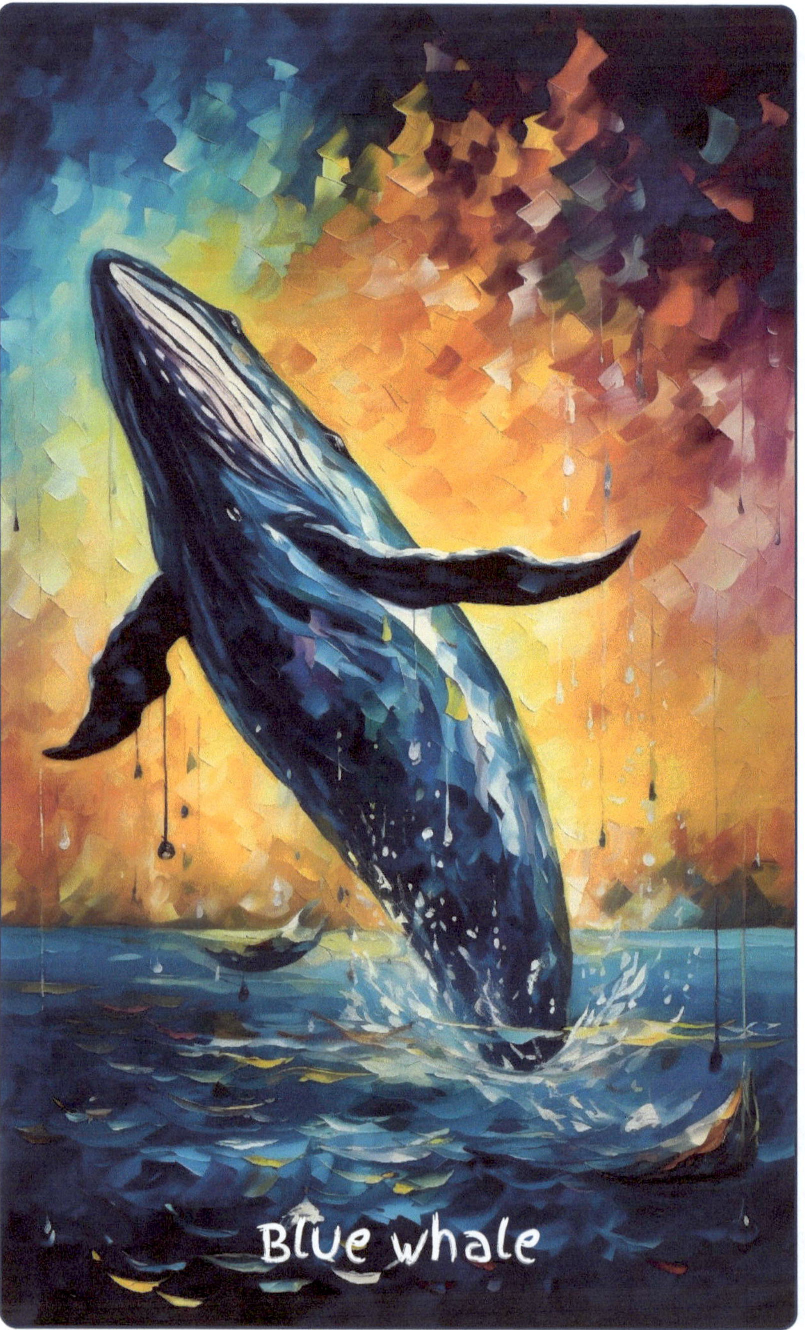

Blue whale

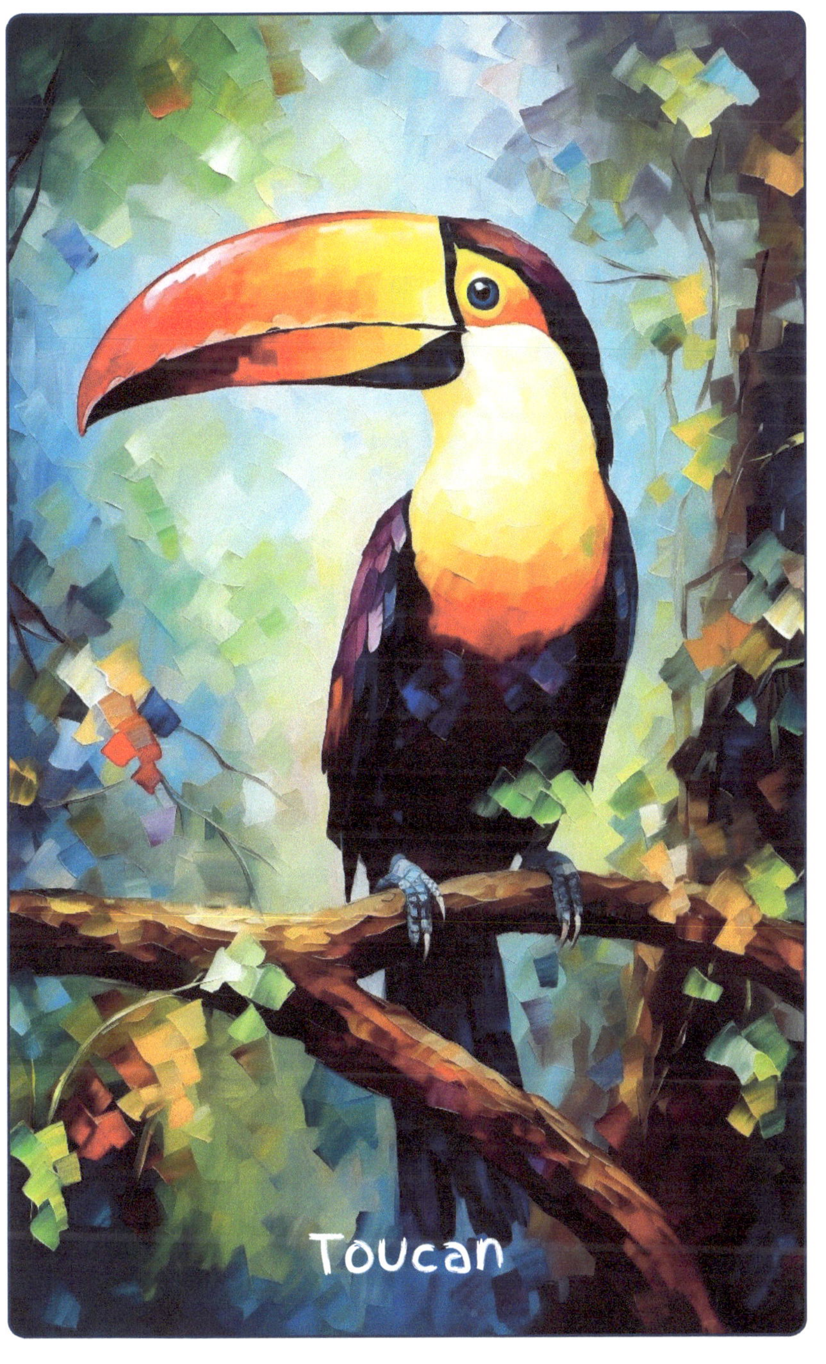
Toucan

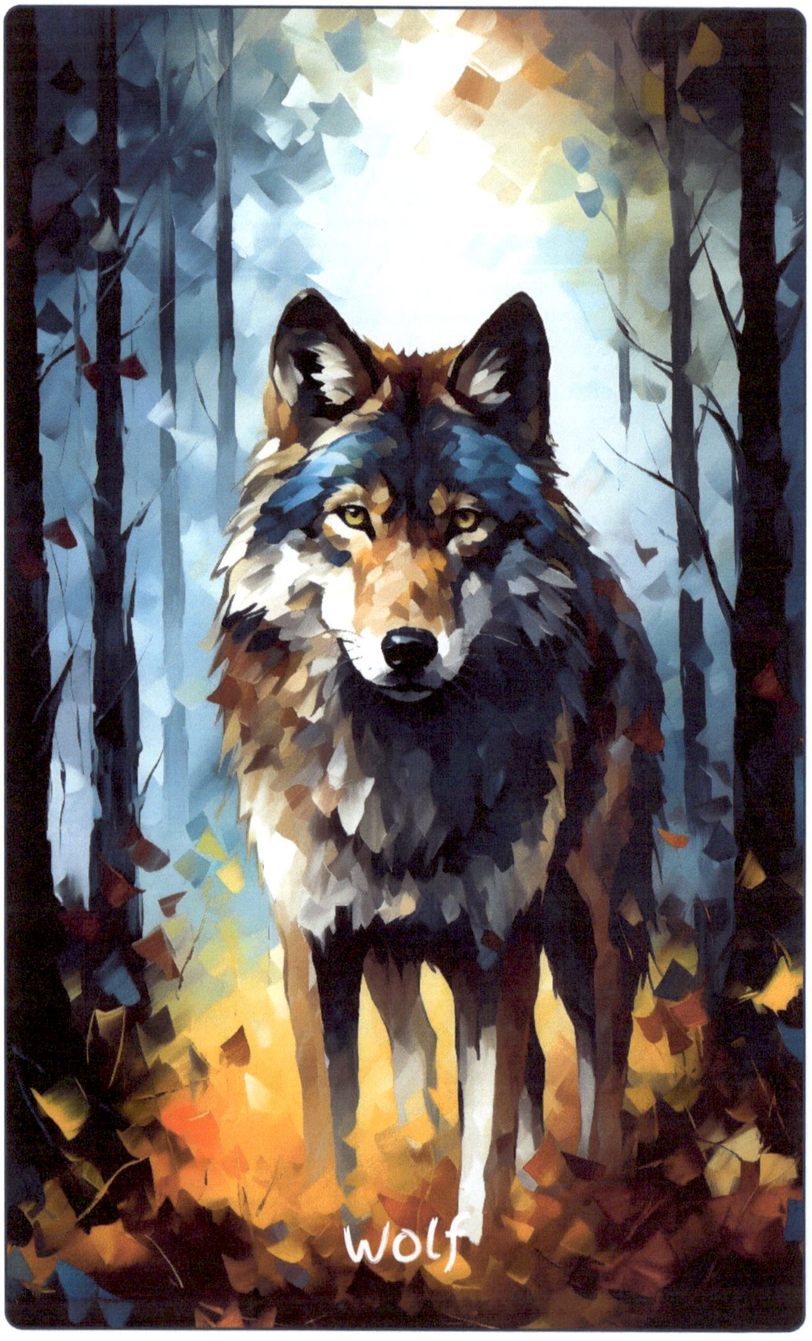

Wolf

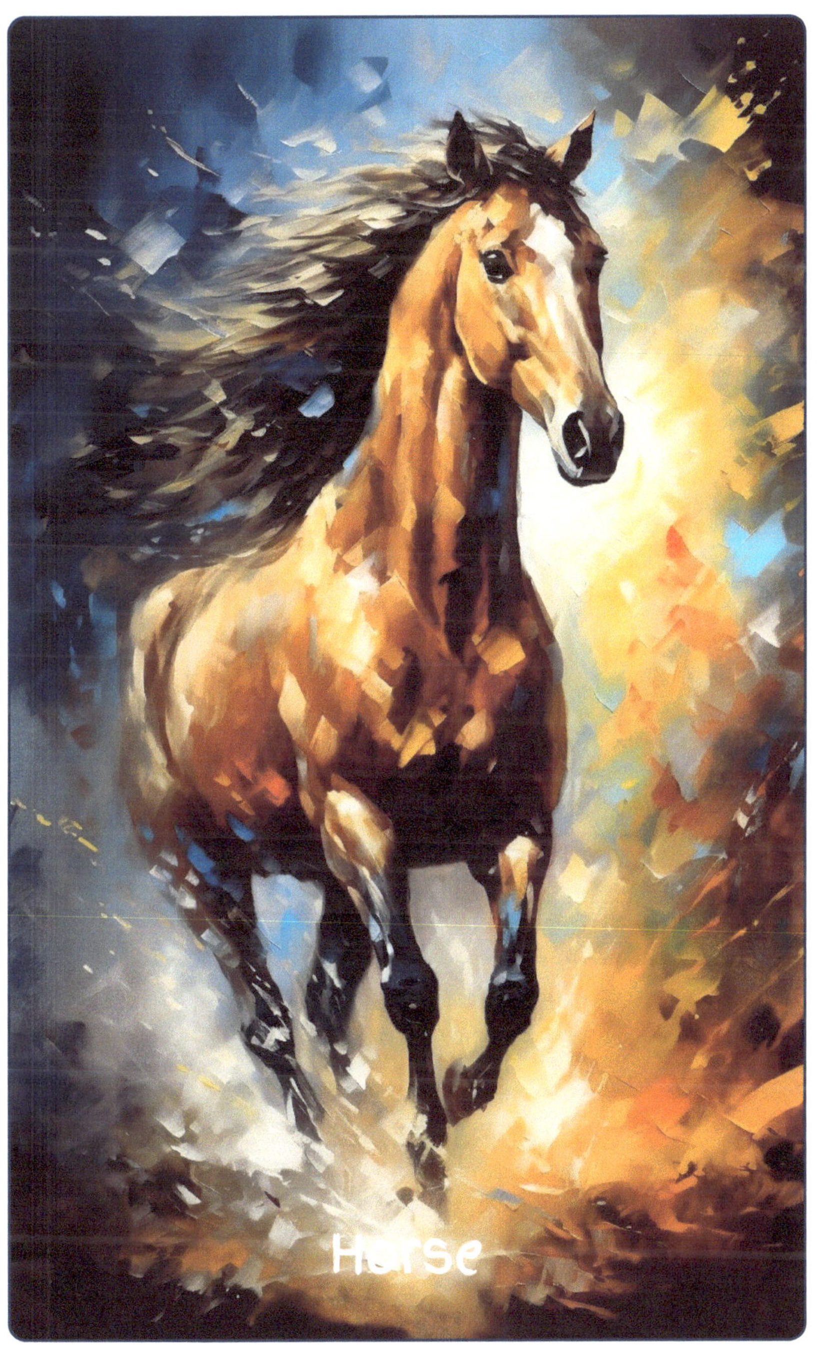
Horse

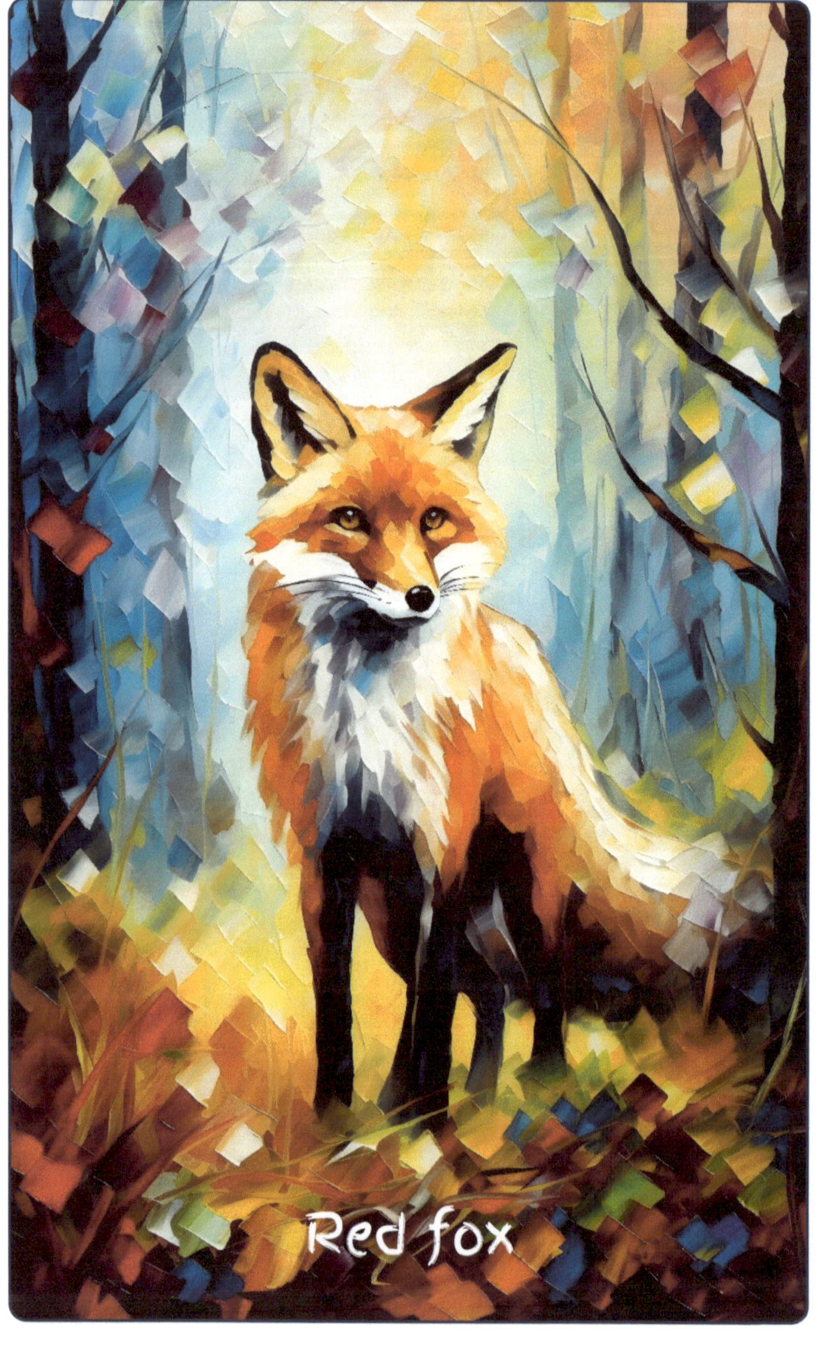
Red fox

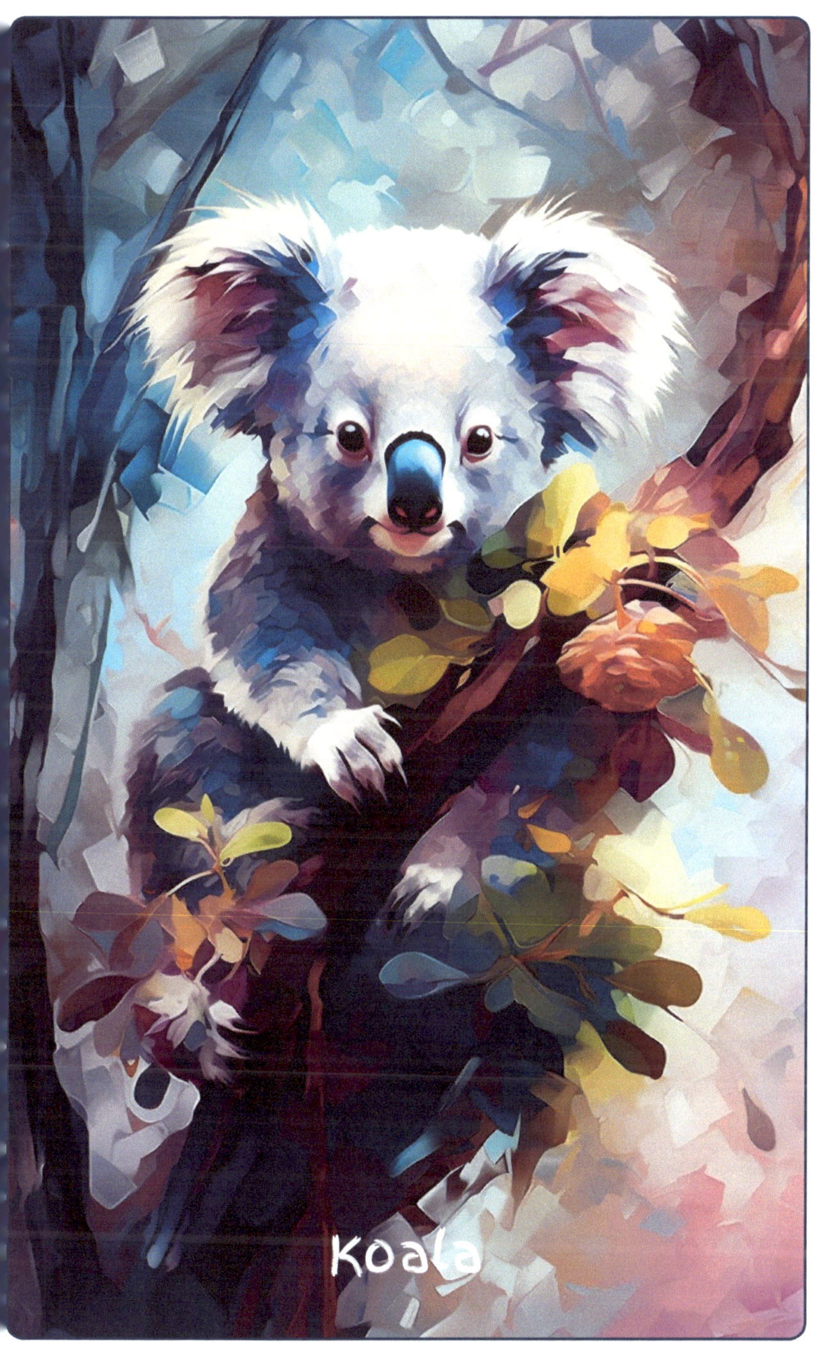
Koala

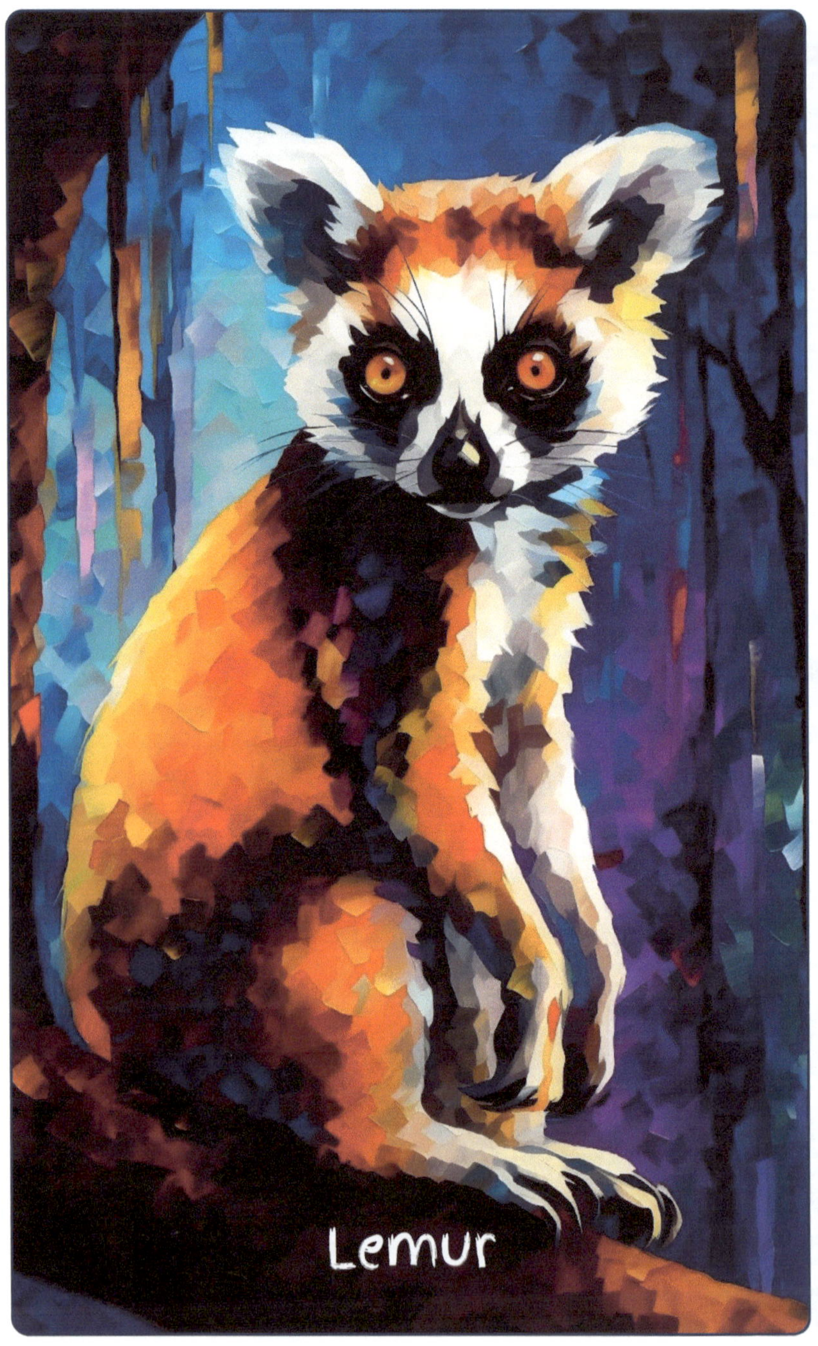
Lemur

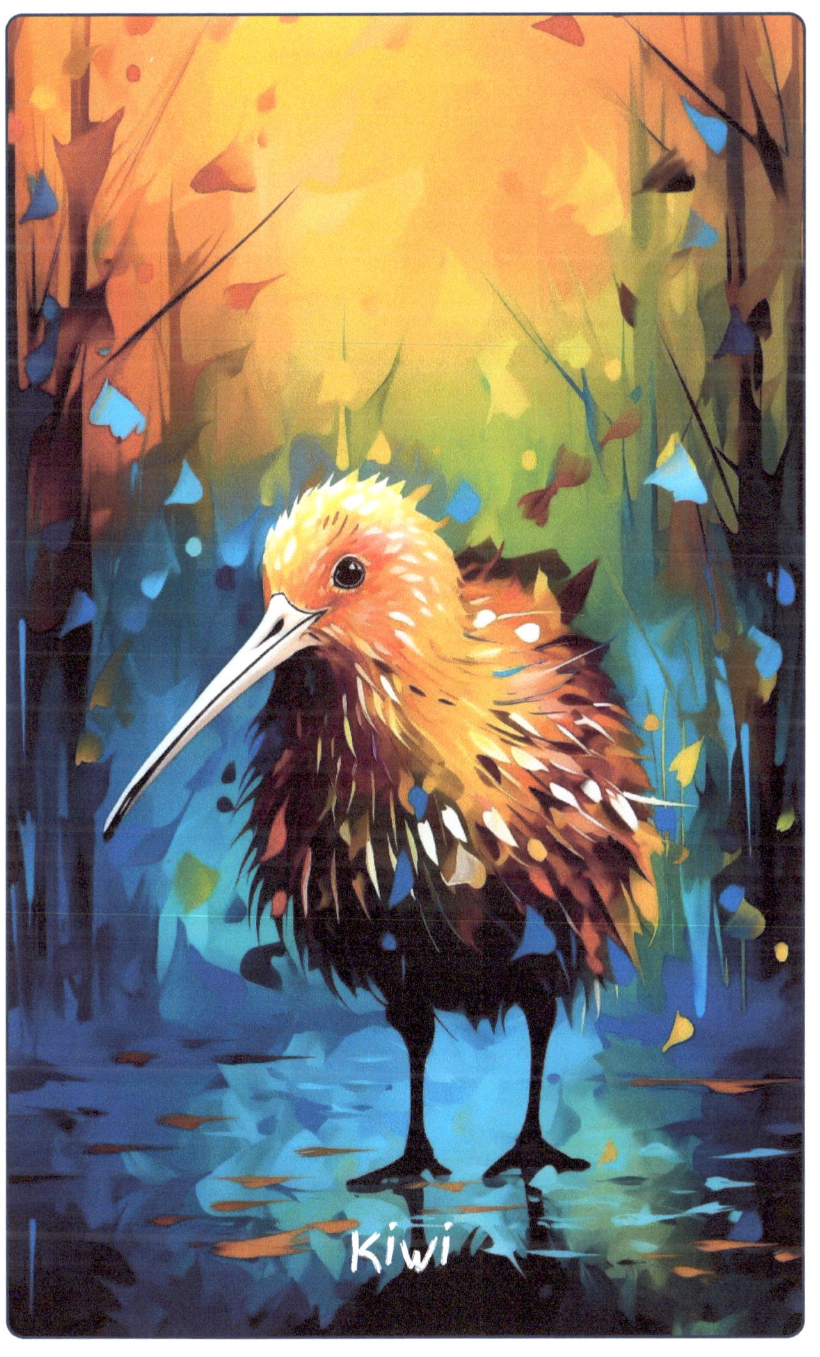
Kiwi

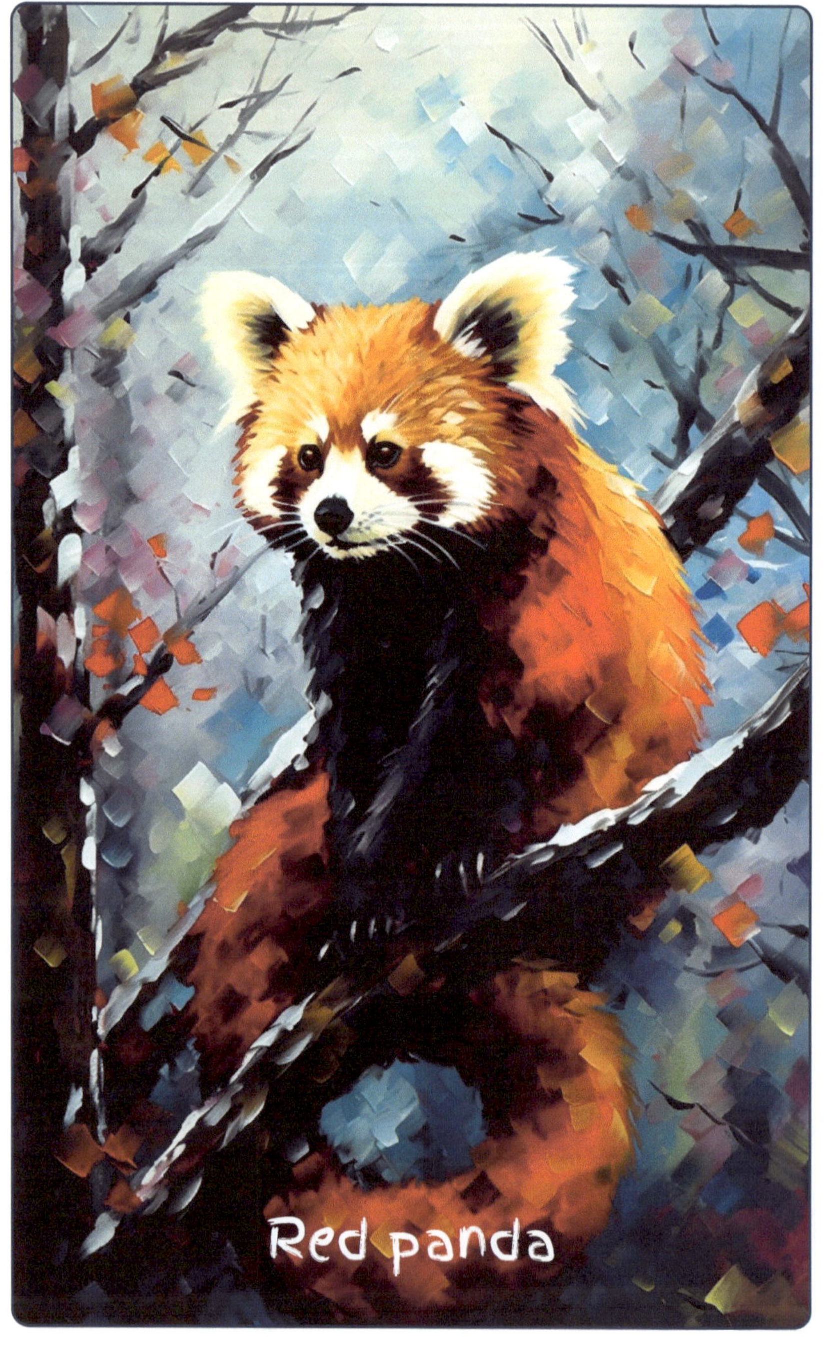

Red panda

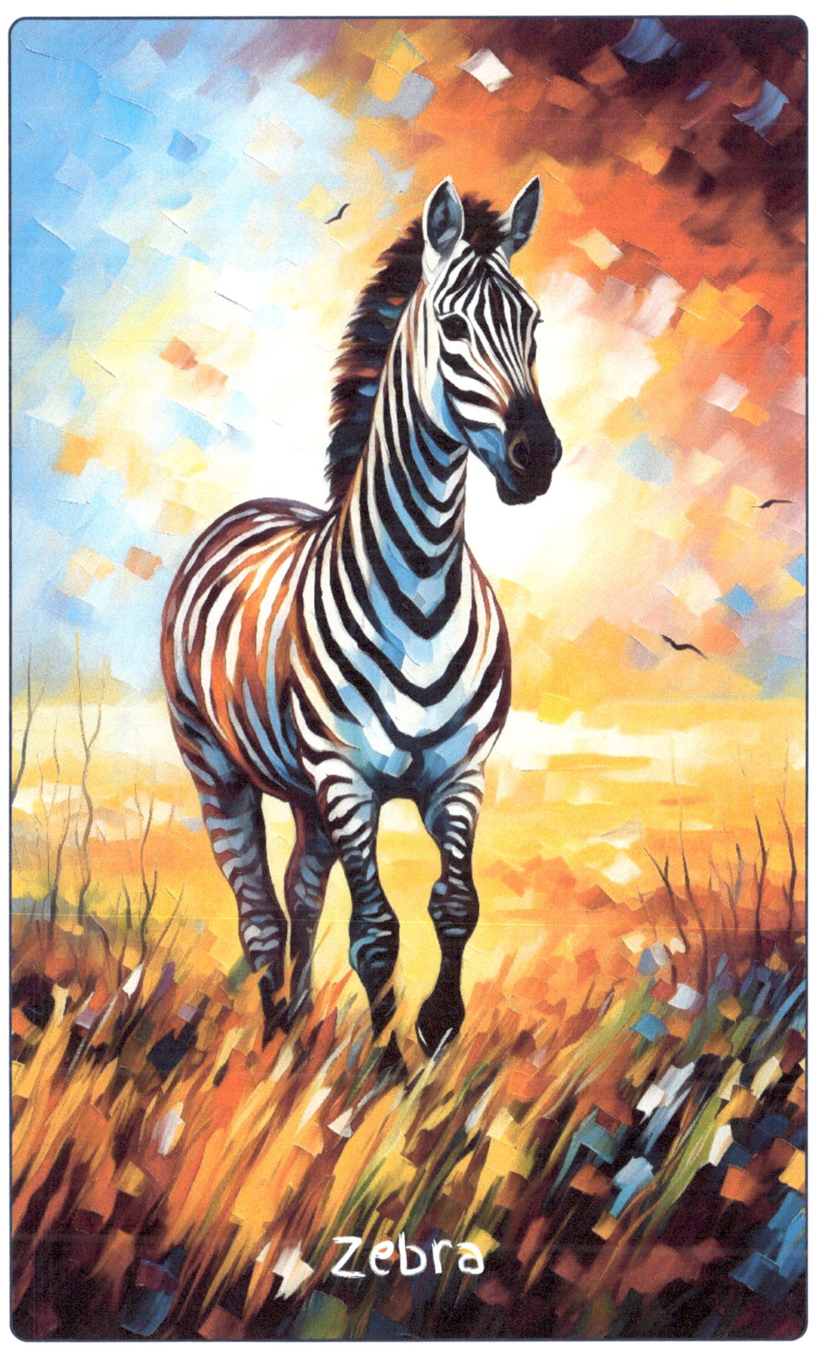

Zebra

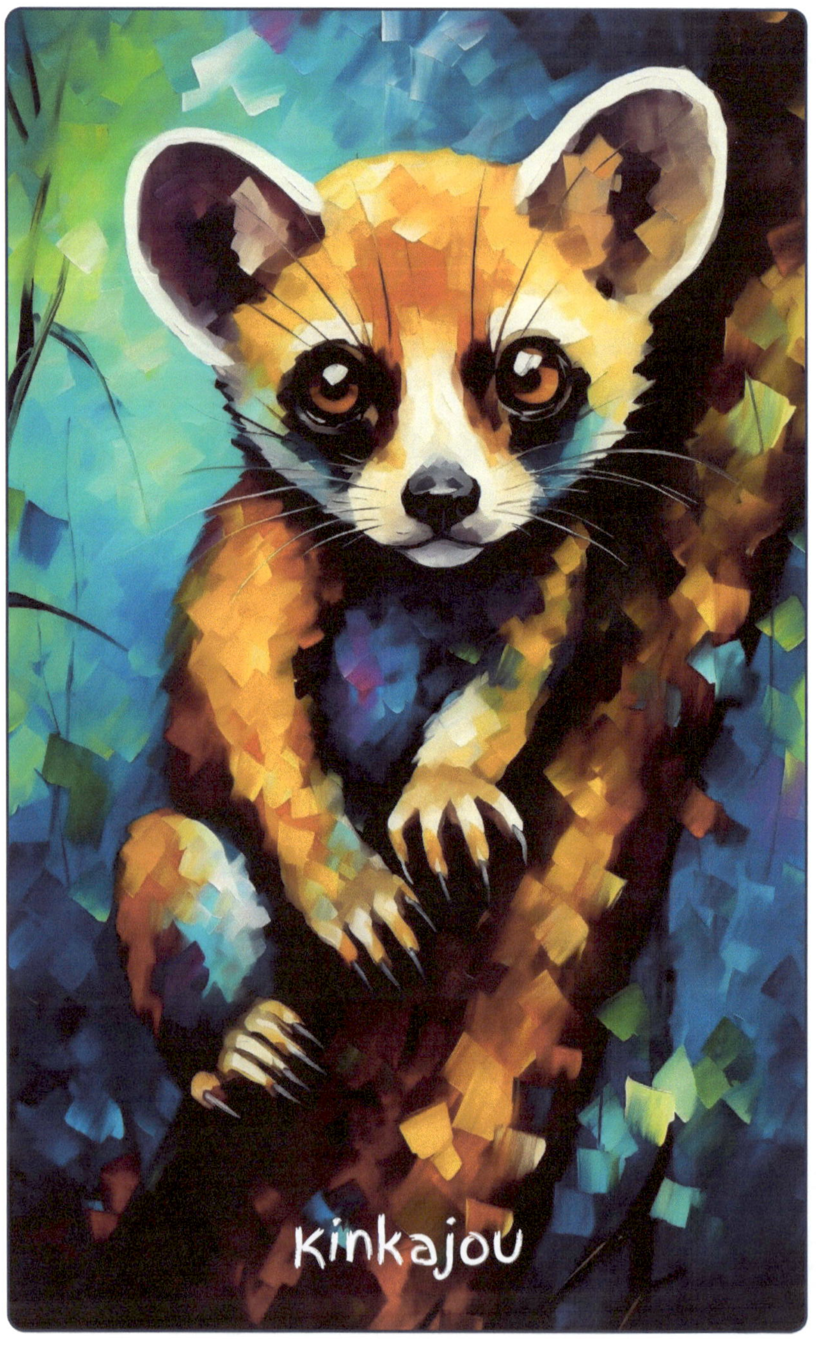

Kinkajou

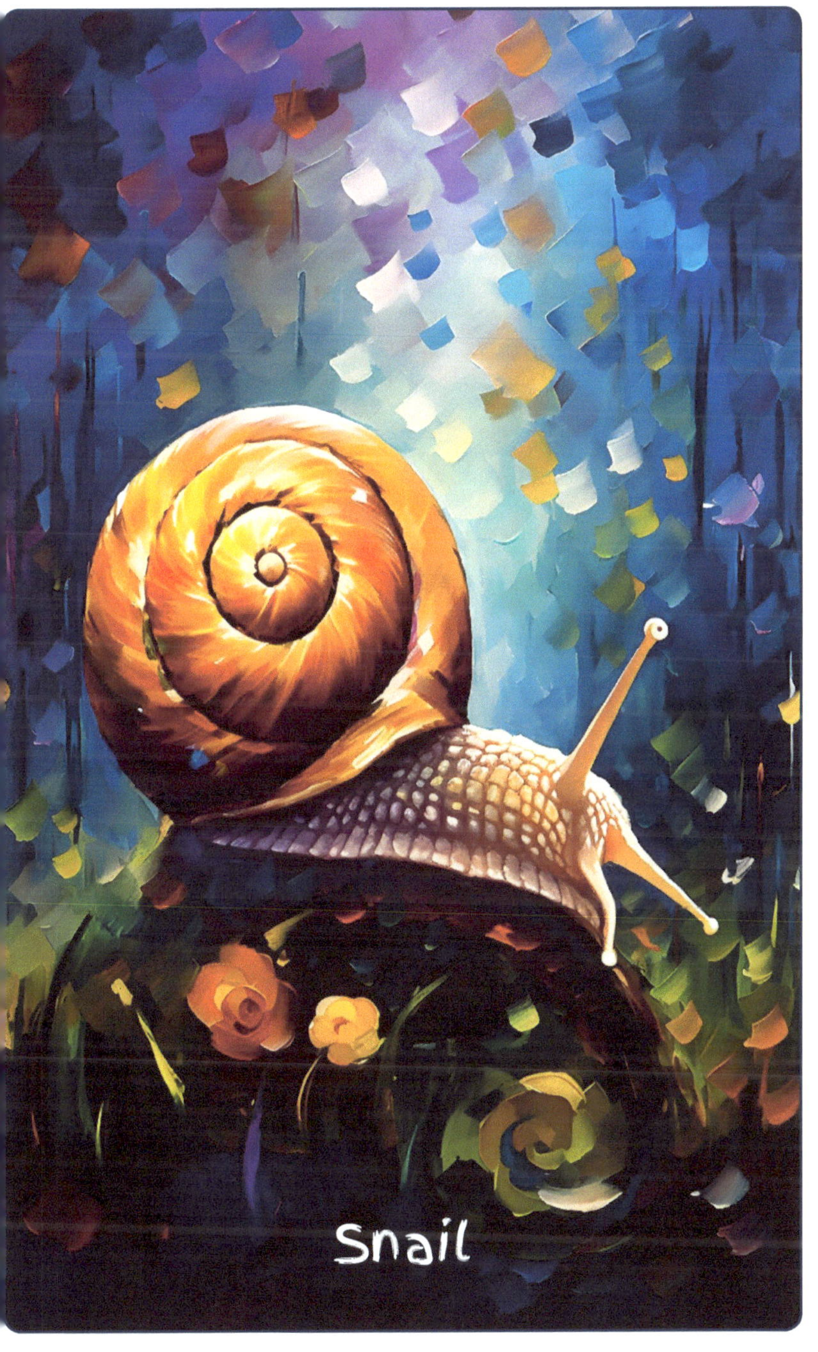

Snail

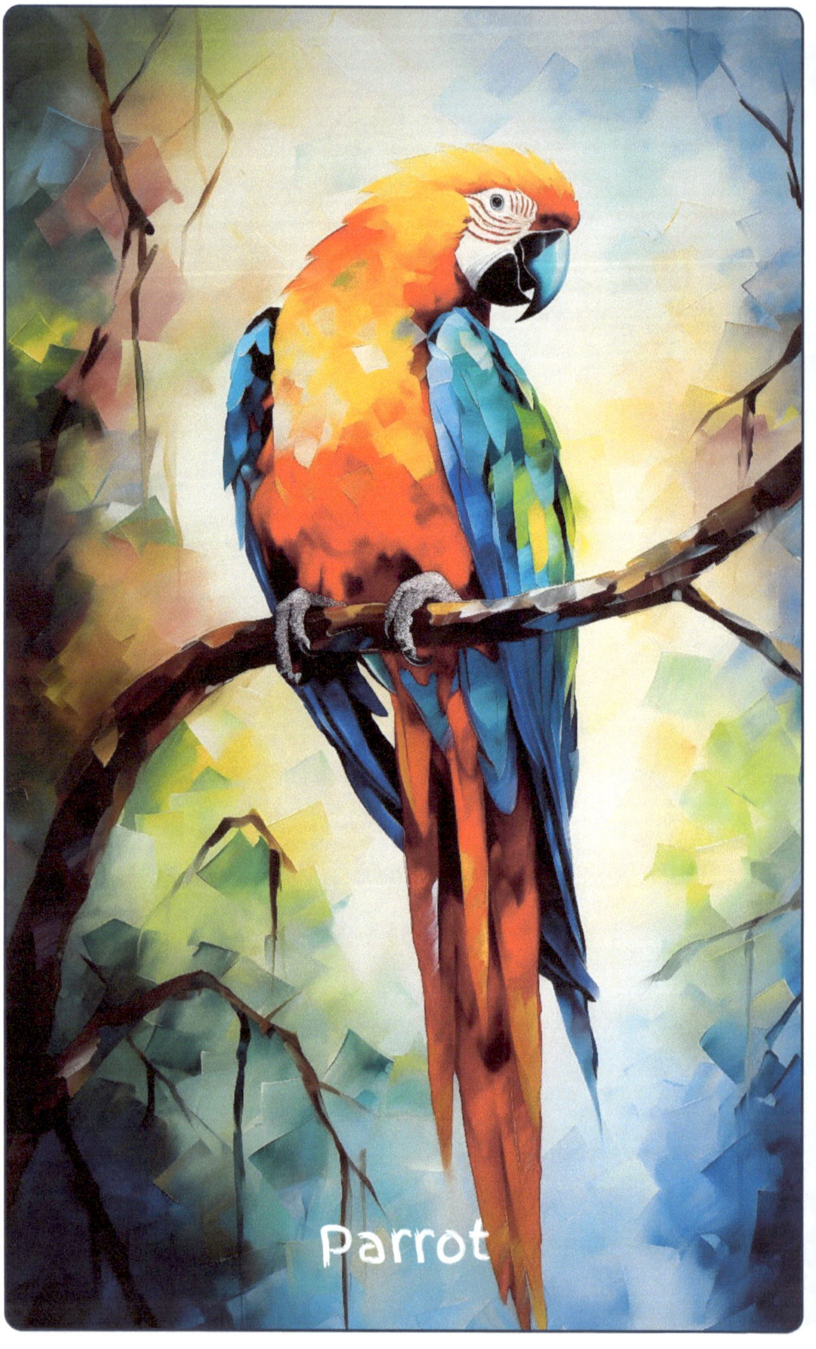

Parrot

If you enjoy this book, please consider leaving a positive review on Amazon.

Thank you :)

<u>More books available on Amazon.com</u>

- **"Famous in STEM" collection:**

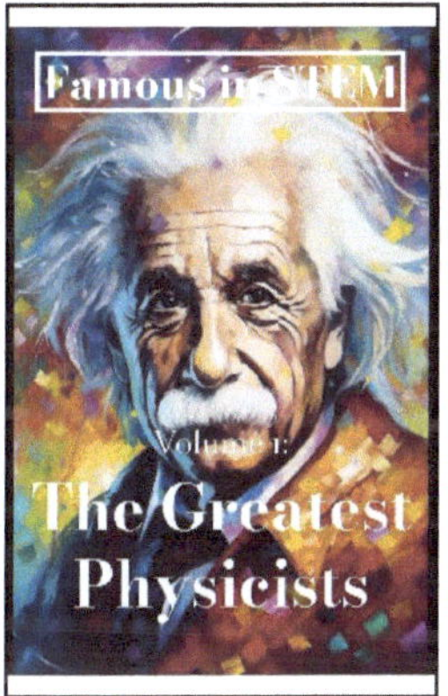

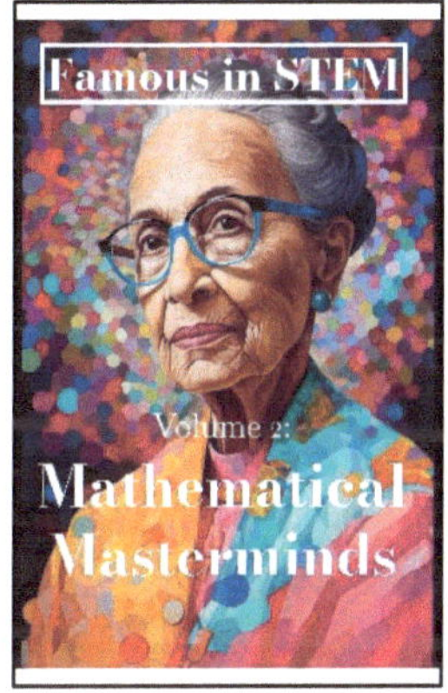

- **"200 Jobs Explained: The Ultimate Career Guide. Discover the career of your dreams with 200 career profiles to explore"**

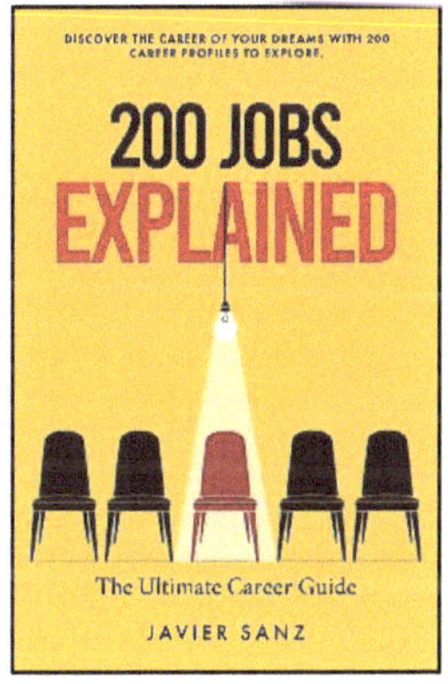

- **"The Motorcycle Picture Book: Amazing illustrations of all types of motorcycles"**

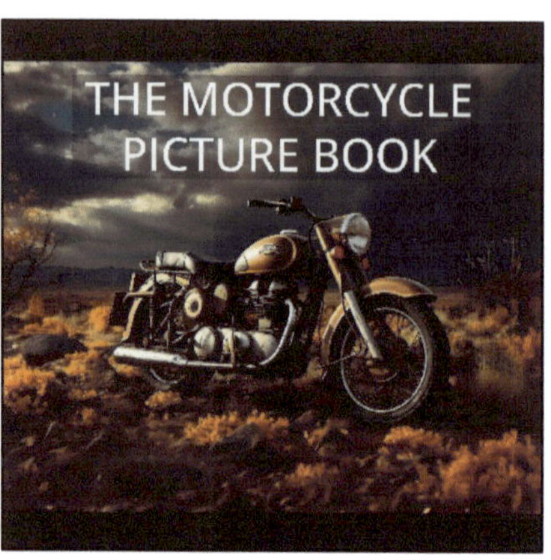

- **"Excel Tips And Tricks: Answers The Top Excel Questions On The Internet"**

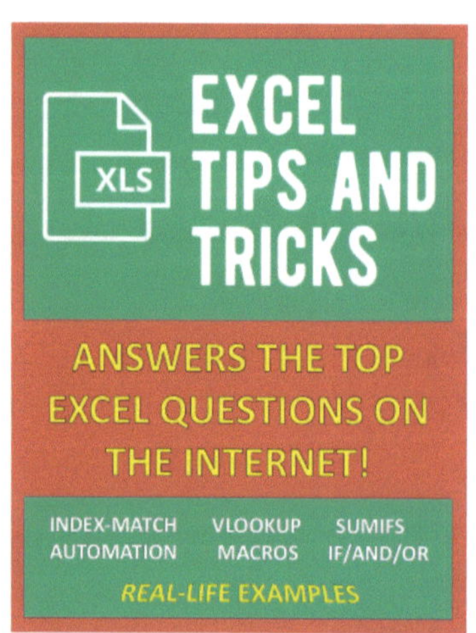